Post-War Europe

A Political Geography

Post-War Europe: A Political Geography
Mark Blacksell

Few would argue that European organizations such as NATO, EFTA, OECD, the EEC, Comecon, and the Warsaw Pact have played an integral part in the political, economic and social development of post-war Europe. Surprisingly few studies, however, have been devoted to the geographical and special contexts of such organizations.

Dr. Blacksell's book is the first study of its type to describe and analyze in straightforward terms the impact of these and other European organizations and institutions on the political geography of the continent as a whole. He sets out to answer such questions as: why has the movement toward economic and political integration been so active in both Western and Eastern Europe since 1945; what did the various organizations set out to do and what had they achieved by the mid-1970s; what is the future of European political integration? The underlying argument is that the emergence of non-European organizations and supranational institutions is the key to a proper understanding of the continent's recent social and economic geography.

Mark Blacksell holds a doctorate in philosophy from Balliol College, Oxford University. He currently teaches geography at the University of Exeter, and has taught also at Columbia University and the University of Southern Illinois.

Post-War Europe

Europe

A Political Geography

Mark Blacksell

Westview Press
Boulder, Colorado

Published in 1977 in Great Britain by
Wm. Dawson and Sons, Ltd.
Cannon House, Folkestone, Kent

Published in 1978 in the United States of America by
Westview Press, Inc.
5500 Central Avenue
Boulder, Colorado 80301
Frederick A. Praeger, Publisher and Editorial Director
© Mark Blacksell

Library of Congress Cataloging in Publication Data

Blacksell, M.   1942–
  Post-war Europe.
  Bibliography: p.
  Includes index.
  1. Europe—Economic conditions—1945–   I. Title.
HC240.B57   330.9'4'055   77–82814
ISBN 0–89158–822–1

Printed litho in Great Britain
by W & J Mackay Ltd, Chatham

Contents

5

Figures

Tables

Preface

European integration is a social, economic and political fact of life for the present generation of students. They have grown up with the EEC, NATO and all the other pan-European organizations, accepting them as part of the fabric of the post-war world. Unfortunately, however, few of them seem to appreciate the antecedents of these organizations, or their precise terms of reference. This book is an attempt to redress that balance. It tries to explain, in the most straightforward terms, why the movement towards European integration has recently been so active, and what it is that the various institutions have been trying to achieve. I hope that it will provide a useful background to the lively debate presently being conducted by geographers into the spatial implications of these changes.

Although I alone am responsible for the book and all its shortcomings, I want to thank the many people who have given their help and advice as I have struggled to put pen to paper. In particular I should like to thank my colleagues in the Geography Department at Exeter University. I also want to pay tribute to Pat Taylor who drew all the maps with a skill that I both envy and admire.

MARK BLACKSELL
January 1977

1

The Dimensions of Change

Political Geography and the New Europe

Since the end of the Second World War in 1945 Europe has undergone a period of unprecedented political, social and economic change.
European supremacy and leadership have not only been seriously
questioned, but in many important respects practically usurped, and
worldwide acceptance of the continent's basic cultural ideas and
standards can no longer even be assumed, let alone taken for granted.
Inside Europe the response has been a fundamental regrouping,
preserving a veneer of independence for the twenty-seven nation
states within its borders, but in reality dividing them into two crude
blocs with widely divergent political ideologies, either side of the Iron
Curtain. Within this wider political and economic framework, the
individual states have been forced progressively to accept co-operation
as the price of ensuring their own political and economic survival. The
North Atlantic and Warsaw Treaty Organizations, the European
Community, the European Free Trade Association and the Council
for Mutual Economic Assistance are all tangible manifestations of the
response to a changed post-war world.

The geographical importance of the new order is immense, for the
structure of the political environment is as fundamental for understanding spatial patterns of human activity as the physical environment. A. E. Moodie claims that the evolution of political structures,
together with the relationship between community and the physical
environment, should be the chief concern of political geography, yet
there are few analyses of the geographical significance of recent
political developments within Europe.[1] There is certainly no contemporary counterpart to Isaiah Bowman's survey *The New World*.[2]

11

This book, first published in 1921, was a geographer's view of the world after the Treaty of Versailles and the peace settlement at the end of the First World War. It was enormously successful, not only among geographers but among all students of world affairs and, subsequently, had to be revised several times to take account of further developments in the inter-war period. However, in the fifty years since it first appeared the book has dated badly. Most of the major empires and many of the individual countries to which it refers no longer exist. The whole pattern of political and economic allegiances has radically altered, yet there are few contemporary studies assessing the geographical impact of these changes, even on a more modest scale.

The reluctance of contemporary geographers to include regional political assessments in their writings is a sad and, in many respects, a damaging omission. The nature of political structures varies from one part of the world to another and, as Muir has pointed out, the now ubiquitous sovereign state is essentially a product of European evolution.[3] Yet despite its fundamental importance in the majority of regional geographies of Europe the treatment of political trends has usually been brief in comparison with the importance attached to historical and physical geography. A text which fails to take detailed account of basic physiography and historical evolution is almost unthinkable, but it is commonplace for the major international European institutions to be either mentioned only in passing, or consigned to an appendix.

The specialist political geographies are not a great deal more helpful, but for different reasons. The problem here is that they are almost all mainly concerned with the general principles and philosophy of political geography, rather than with the regional impact of political events. Where post-war political developments in Europe are mentioned at all, there is not usually much more than a sketch of the bare bones of the new order. Little or no attempt is made to analyse the precise aims and objectives of the new supranational organizations and, more important, their success in realizing them. As a result it is invariably hard to assess their impact on the social and economic geography of individual states.

A more fundamental difficulty is the weight still frequently accorded by geographers to out of date theories of political interaction. The most glaring example of this is the almost obligatory lip-service still paid to Sir Halford J. Mackinder's Heartland theory. His classic and, for its time, extremely penetrating theory about the influence of geography on the world political order in *Democratic Ideals and Reality* was first published in 1919 and, by his own admission, was based on ideas he had developed well before the First World War.[4] Concepts such as the Europe-centred World Island, Heartland and the rigid division of the seaman's and the landsman's points of view were all evolved in an era before modern technology, especially new developments in transportation, had reshaped the whole pattern of global communications. The automobile and the aeroplane have not only reduced the impact of sheer physical distance, they have given new meaning and strength to political alliances between widely separated nations and states.

Mackinder's views were controversial when they were first published, but despite being repeatedly challenged in the intervening period, they are still allowed to form a basis for argument. The ghost seems never to be completely laid. Even the most fundamental and dismissive critiques, like that meted out by S. B. Cohen, fail to completely bury the earlier arguments, largely because their alternative scenarios are themselves not entirely convincing.[5] In Cohen's case his basic division of the world into two major geostrategic regions, the Trade-Dependent Maritime World and the Eurasian Continental World, divided by two shatter belts in the Middle East and Southeast Asia, seems to fit the facts of the contemporary world political situation quite neatly, but his analysis of the territorial needs of a resurgent Europe is much less plausible. He believes that Europe's major strategic weakness lies in the lack of variety and extent of its territory, and he suggests that a more viable unit would be the combination of Maritime Europe and the Maghreb in North Africa. It is this concentration on the importance of territory *per se* for explaining the distribution of political and economic power, which has been a continuous and somewhat misleading thread in political geography, from Mackinder to Cohen and beyond. Taking Cohen's particular case, anything approaching integration between Europe and North Africa seems unlikely either immediately, or in the longer-term. In the ten years since the book was written, most of the North African states have aligned themselves strongly with the Arab world, but Europe's political and economic stature in global terms has still been greatly enhanced. By acting more in concert the European states have realized the extent of their own political and economic strength and, contrary to Cohen's contention, they have not been notably inhibited by a lack of the vast open spaces and free territory available to both the United States and the Soviet Union.

The main argument in this book is that the internal political developments in post-war Europe, particularly the emergence of pan-European organizations and supranational institutions, are one of the keys to a proper understanding of the continent's social and economic geography. Nevertheless, one must always be mindful of the danger of being overtaken by events. A sudden change of leadership, such as occurred in Portugal in 1975, or the development of a new resource, like North Sea oil, can radically alter the whole basis of political decision-making. There is, however, some reason for believing that Europe has settled into a new and more stable period in its history: the adjustments to political boundaries made necessary by the results of the Second World War are now complete,[6] and the

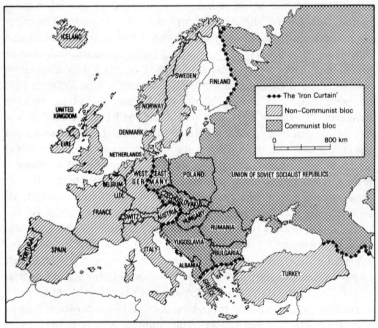

Figure 1   The division of Europe by the Iron Curtain

direct intervention of the United States and the Soviet Union in European affairs has been superseded by European organizations, dominated by the European countries themselves, rather than the two super-powers. After more than thirty years of uncertainty, the political order seems more permanent and, although it is certain that changes will occur in the membership of the various supranational organizations, the future of the organizations themselves and their decisive role in European affairs seems assured in the foreseeable future.

The European Organizations

In any consideration of international groupings in the post-war continent of Europe, the most fundamental division is the ideological one between the Communist peoples' democracies in the east and the politically more varied nations in the north, west and south. As can be seen from Figure 1, the two groups are neatly divided from one another physically. Finland is the only state under the direct political influence of both camps, a result of its close physical and cultural links with the rest of Scandinavia and its strategic importance to the Soviet Union. When it is remembered that the so-called Iron Curtain, which divides the two groups, stretches overland for nearly 1,500 kilometres, the rigidity and completeness is really quite remarkable. The terrain covered makes for easy contact along the greater part of its length, yet contact has been minimal, highly regimented and confined to a handful of crossing points. After more than thirty years during which time there has been no European war, all interchange still requires high level government sanction, and unofficial contacts are strictly illegal. The latter are also sufficiently rare to continue to be treated as items of news by the western press. Despite the gradual relaxation of political tension at an official governmental level between the two sides, there are still no real signs of any more general rapprochement. The Iron Curtain remains one of the most powerful geographical barriers in continental Europe.

This fundamental division is naturally reflected in all the international organizations and groupings in the continent, for the origins of most of them are rooted in the ideological conflict between the Communist and the non-Communist worlds. The most pervasive and all-embracing of these organizations is the Organization for Economic Co-operation and Development (OECD) (see Figure 2), which includes all the west European states together with other non-European members (Australia, Canada, Japan and the United States). They are pledged to promote the general expansion of world trade by encouraging the economic development of its members and by taking active steps to raise standards in the developing world. The OECD grew out of the Organization for European Economic Co-operation, which was set up at the insistence of the United States to guide the immediate post-war reconstruction of the west European economy. Both organizations have played a crucial role in co-ordinating the economic affairs of a varied group of nations, but in neither case has their role extended beyond this to any form of political integration. There is no attempt to undermine or water down the principle of national

	West European Union	European Community	European Free Trade Association	North Atlantic Treaty Organisation	Council of Europe	Organisation for Economic Co-operation and Development
Belgium	★	★		★	★	★
Netherlands	★	★		★	★	★
Luxembourg	★	★		★	★	★
Italy	★	★		★	★	★
France	★	★		★	★	★
West Germany	★	★		★	★	★
United Kingdom	★	★		★	★	★
Eire		☆			★	★
Denmark		☆		★	★	★
Norway		☆	★	★	★	★
Sweden			★		★	★
Iceland			★	★	★	★
Austria			★		★	★
Switzerland			★		★	★
Portugal			★	★		★
Greece				★	★	★
Turkey				★	★	★
Finland			◄			★
Malta					★	★
Cyprus					★	
Spain						★
Yugoslavia						○

★ Denotes member   ☆ Denotes new member   ◄ Denotes associate member   ○ Denotes observer

The United States, Canada, Japan and Australia are also members of the Organisation for Economic Co-operation and Development, New Zealand is an observer.
The United States and Canada are also members of the North Atlantic Treaty Organisation.

Figure 2   Membership of international and supranational organizations in Europe 1977

sovereignty. In the European Community on the other hand the ultimate aim is supranational government. The Community was formed in 1967 by amalgamating three separate existing bodies, the European Coal and Steel Community, the European Economic Community and Euratom. The European Coal and Steel Community was the first to be formed in 1952, with Belgium, France, Italy, Luxembourg, the Netherlands and West Germany as its founder members. In 1958 the same countries banded together again to form the other two bodies. The aim of all three was to promote progressive economic integration as a means of eventually achieving greater political unity. Merging the executives of the three bodies in 1967 to form a single European Community was a step in this direction. In 1972 the Community was enlarged to include Denmark, Eire and the United Kingdom, and in 1977 applications are pending from Greece, Spain and Portugal.

Other west European countries have definitely decided against membership of the European Community, because they feel it would compromise their political or economic independence, or both. In 1960 some of them came together to form the European Free Trade Association, an organization with none of the long-term political aims and supranational institutions of the European Community. The European Free Trade Association exists merely to facilitate the gradual elimination of all restrictions on trade in industrial goods between its members. At present, in 1977, the organization is more or less moribund, although Austria, Iceland, Norway, Portugal, Sweden and Switzerland are still nominally members and Finland is an associate member. The European Free Trade Association has never really recovered from the loss of its largest member, the United Kingdom, together with Denmark, to the European Community in 1972.

If economic advantage has been one important stimulus for integration, the other has been defence. However, the west European defence agreements are rather more exclusive than their economic counterparts. The largest and most important is the North Atlantic Treaty Organization, signed in 1948 by ten European countries (see Figure 2), together with the United States and Canada. Greece and Turkey were admitted in 1951 and West Germany became a member in 1954. The aim of the North Atlantic Treaty Organization is straightforward. The founding treaty states that an attack by an outside power on any one of the member states will be construed as an attack against them all and result in a concerted military response. Fortunately these brave words have never yet been put to the test, but the organization has been a major cohesive force in western Europe. It has resulted in joint defence planning for more than a generation and prevented the development of smaller, more exclusive military alliances in western Europe. The only other defence agreement of note is the West European Union, which was formally inaugurated in 1955, but in practice is little more than a forum where the Foreign Ministers of Belgium, France, Italy, Luxembourg, the Netherlands, the United Kingdom and West Germany can meet together to discuss common defence problems. Anything decided by the West European Union has to be implemented within the framework of the North Atlantic Treaty Organization.

Finally mention must be made of the most general and potentially furthest-reaching of all the west European political organizations, the Council of Europe. It was established in 1949 with the aim of achieving 'a greater unity between its members for the purpose of safeguarding and realizing the ideals which are their common heritage and facilitating their economic and social progress'.[7] The importance of the Council of Europe is less its direct political and economic achievements, which have been relatively modest, but rather the acceptance it symbolizes among the seventeen member nations (see Figure 2), that there is in western Europe a common heritage and a social fabric worth cherishing. Although the role of the Council is purely advisory and members are not technically bound by any of its decisions, it has still managed to play an important role in establishing common standards of conduct, especially in the field of human rights. The history of Greece's relations with the Council is indicative of the high regard in which it is held. During the seven years that Greece was under military dictatorship, between 1968 and 1975, the country's membership was suspended. One of the first acts of the new democratically elected government was to apply for readmission.

In eastern Europe the pattern of international co-operation has been quite different and, in general, much less complex. All eight of the Communist-ruled peoples' democracies have individual treaties with the Soviet Union both for defence and economic matters. Their powerful eastern neighbour therefore dominates the broader international agreements in a way that the United States could not and would not want to do in western Europe. As can be seen from Figure 3, the two truly international organizations in eastern Europe are the Council for Mutual Economic Assistance (Comecon) and the Warsaw Treaty Organization. Comecon was founded in 1949 as a Soviet counter to the political and economic involvement of the United States in the post-war reconstruction of western Europe. Since then the organization has evolved to become one of the chief channels for co-ordinating economic development in eastern Europe. The original signatories were Bulgaria, Czechoslovakia, Hungary, Poland, Rumania and the Soviet Union, but this caucus was subsequently expanded to include Albania and East Germany, with Yugoslavia as an observer. In addition there were also a few non-European Communist countries, which were either members or observers. The treaty setting up the Warsaw Treaty Organization was signed in 1955 by the

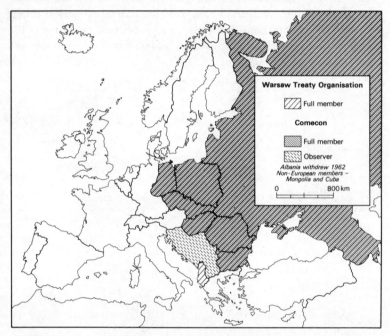

Figure 3   Membership of Comecon and the Warsaw Treaty Organization 1977

European members of Comecon and the Soviet Union, but not by Yugoslavia. Once again the initial stimulus was the need to provide a formal counter to a development in western Europe, in this case the admission of the Federal Republic of Germany to the North Atlantic Treaty Organization. Given the existing bilateral treaties between the Soviet Union and all the east European Communist states, it initially added little to the existing network of defence agreements. Gradually however, it has begun to assume a more central role, ensuring that none of its members broke ranks in the fight to preserve a communist buffer zone between the Soviet Union and western Europe. The brutal reality of this role was brought forcefully home by the invasion of Czechoslovakia by Soviet, East German, Polish and Hungarian troops, acting under the authority of the Warsaw Treaty Organization, in 1968.

These then are the main organizations in both eastern and western Europe, that have produced the new patterns of political, social and economic interaction in the continent since 1945 and they are the main focus of this book. Naturally they have not worked in isolation. Physical circumstances, historical accident and economic advantage, not to mention the cultural heritage of the individual nation states, remain fundamental considerations for a proper understanding of the continent's geography and growth. The point is that no longer are they the only ones.

2

Battleground Europe and the Passing of Mitteleuropa

The Demise of Central Europe as a Political Force

The present political pattern in Europe is largely a result of the manoeuvrings of the Allies during the final stages of the Second World War and it bears all the chaotic marks of that period.[1] By 1945 all the Allied governments were so concerned with achieving an unconditional German surrender that none gave anything but the most minimal consideration to the likely long-term consequences of the peace. Suddenly, as Germany collapsed, they were faced with the monumental task of welding the fragments of the Third Reich into a new Europe. It was a task from which there was no escape and to which they had radically different solutions. Richard Mayne put the dilemma succinctly, when he wrote that 'Hitler, by destroying the old Europe, had destroyed the Allies' isolation and brought them face to face. The crippling of France and the impoverishment of Great Britain ensured that the confrontation was essentially between America and the Soviet Union'.[2] This confrontation has since dominated the social, economic and political life of every European country and it is the background against which all the reconstruction of the past thirty years has occurred.

The most important fact of the post-war upheaval is the demise of central Europe as a political force in its own right. As Eric Fischer pointed out in his seminal paper 'The passing of Mitteleuropa', the new order whittled away the heterogeneous bloc of independent nation states that previously formed the core of the continent, until all that remained was the thin, continuous line of the Iron Curtain with its complement of military guards, barbed wire and mines.[3] It symbolized the apparent impossibility of reconciling two opposing

21

ideologies. The rampant and belligerent expansion of three successive German Reichs had been brought to an abrupt halt, pre-1939 allegiances had been rendered meaningless and nations were forced to look elsewhere for mutual support. In the majority of cases they had no choice in the matter: in 1945 the independence of all the countries in central Europe was revoked forthwith and each found itself un-equivocally under the wing of either the Soviet Union, or the United States and its European allies. Not even those few countries, such as Finland, Austria and Yugoslavia, who formed the buffer zone between the two, could enjoy full independence; they simply had to cope with pressures from both sides.

Obviously the main aim of the Allies throughout the Second World War was to defeat the Axis powers, but for some there was also a sizeable underlying streak of territorial greed.[4] The final resolution of their competing claims is a fascinating, if rather confusing story, achieved by a combination of political collusion and military tact in the final stages of the war. Of all the major Allied countries the Soviet Union had suffered most from the territorial ambitions of the Third Reich and it is, therefore, not surprising that it was keenest to see the balance redressed, or even weighted in its favour. From the moment he agreed to enter the war Stalin made it clear that in return for helping the United Kingdom, France and the United States win the war, he wanted complete freedom to dominate eastern Europe, so that he could create a deeper and more secure frontier for the Soviet Union. Tacit agreement for the principle was forthcoming from the outset and, at a meeting in Moscow between Churchill, Roosevelt and Stalin in October 1944, the three leaders informally discussed the logistic implications of the understanding. Churchill and Stalin went even further and drafted the outline of a rough division of Europe. The gist of this was that no attempt should be made to hinder the Russian advance into the Balkans and the Soviet Union should be allowed to keep a 90 per cent interest in Rumania and a 75 per cent interest in Bulgaria; Hungary and Yugoslavia were to be divided equally, but Greece was to remain firmly outside Soviet control. It is not clear whether Roosevelt was a party to these suggestions and it is hard now to assess their ultimate significance, but, even so, it is certain that it was in just this very *ad hoc* sort of manner that the shape of post-war Europe began to be decided.[5]

Naturally such collusion was but a beginning, but it is indicative of the general lack of detailed planning for the aftermath of the war and the air of unreality surrounding what few negotiations there were. Gradually other, more mundane factors began to influence the situation. Most important was the actual pattern of the Allied advance into Europe and the eventual convergence on Germany (Figure 4). The Soviet army, which had been driving inexorably westwards on a broad coherent front since the Battle of Leningrad in 1942, divided into two in the latter part of 1944, mainly to avoid the difficult terrain in the Carpathian mountains, which run from the Ukraine through Czechoslovakia and separate the North German and the Pannomanian plains. In the south its army skirted the Black Sea and

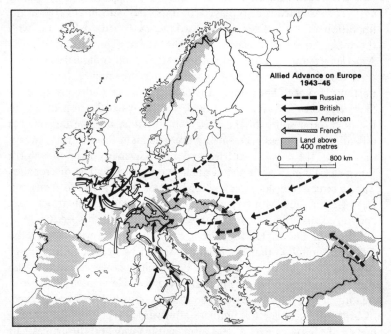

Figure 4   The Allied advance into Germany

penetrated deep into Rumania and Bulgaria, then followed the Danube valley across Hungary and into Austria, via the Vienna Gate. Here it joined forces with the rest of the Russian advance, that had gone north of the mountains and kept to the open country in Poland and Germany. By mid-1945 the pincer movement was complete and presented a more or less united front across Europe, from the Baltic to the Adriatic Seas.

In the west the advance of the American and British troops was on a broader front and was altogether more ponderous and indecisive. The inevitable compromises inherent in a joint command and the more modest territorial ambitions of both the United States and the United Kingdom combined to produce a less ruthlessly single-minded thrust into Germany. The first foothold on the European mainland from the west was achieved when the British invaded Italy and the Balkans from North Africa in 1943. Progress was painfully slow and it was not until the spring of 1945 that the troops were able to penetrate as far north as the Po valley and into Austria. Here the advance halted as it came face to face with the Soviet army marching from the east. The Americans also played an important subsidiary role in the liberation of Italy, their troops striking westward to link up with the main American advance through France. The second British–American front in Europe had been started on 6 June 1944, when their combined forces took part in the Normandy landings in northern France. The Americans crossed France and converged on Germany via the Saverne and Belfort gaps, which lie respectively to the north and south of the Vosges mountains, but the terrain was difficult and progress necessarily slow. The main British army, sweeping across the Low Countries and into Germany over the North European Plain, forged ahead much more quickly. The discrepancy was a source of considerable friction between the British and American High Commands. Montgomery, leading the main British attack, was convinced that the overriding objective ought to be a speedy all-out advance on Berlin. He thought it essential to try and capture the German capital so that the Russians would be denied an important psychological advantage in the developing power struggle. The American commander Eisenhower disagreed. He wanted to proceed steadily across the whole front, so that there would be fewer pockets of isolated resistance to eliminate afterwards. Whatever the relative merits of the two views, Eisenhower had his way and the armies had only reached as far east as the Elbe river, when they met the Russians. The confrontation effectively completed the division of Europe and the basic territorial balance of power has since altered very little, notwithstanding the abortive Communist putsches in Greece and Turkey in 1947. Any semblance of an independent Central Europe, uncommitted to either the United States or the Soviet Union, had certainly disappeared. Troops from the two dominant, opposing factions in the alliance were firmly entrenched, either side of what, in 1945, the German statesman Count Schwerin von Krosigk emotively called the Iron Curtain, and steps were quickly taken to consolidate their respective positions.

The German Question

The first line of the national anthem, adopted by the newly formed Federal Republic of Germany demands 'Unity, justice and freedom for Germany', but its high flown sentiments only serve to highlight the impossibility of achieving such purist goals in the years immediately after the end of the Second World War. Faced with a demoralized population and a nation that for any practical purpose no longer existed, the Allies found that not only had they no common policies, they had virtually no individual policies either.

The only attempt at a comprehensive plan for Germany, published prior to the end of hostilities, was the American Morgenthau Plan (Figure 5).[6] Henry Morgenthau, the United States Secretary of the Treasury in the Roosevelt Administration, took it upon himself to prepare a contingency plan for permanently rendering Germany militarily impotent once the war was over. He was convinced that for the plan to be effective most of the country's industrial plant would have to be confiscated and the urban-industrial population resettled in the countryside and employed in rural occupations. To this end he

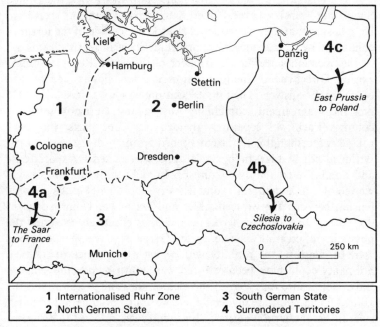

| 1 Internationalised Ruhr Zone | 3 South German State |
| 2 North German State | 4 Surrendered Territories |

Figure 5   The Morgenthau Plan for Germany

proposed that the former Third Reich be divided into two autonomous states, one in the north with Berlin as its capital and the other in the south, based on Munich. He further suggested that the Ruhr conurbation, which he defined as an area stretching from Kiel in the north to Frankfurt am Main in the south, should be made an international zone and administered by the Allies for their own profit. The plan also proposed that Silesia in the east and the Saar in the west be ceded to Czechoslovakia and France respectively.

Morgenthau's plan is less important for its precise detail than for the attitude of mind it represented. Despite the disastrous consequences of the Treaty of Versailles in 1919 and the dire warnings of such eminent people as the economist J. M. Keynes about the dangers of economically and socially isolating a defeated Germany,[7] the prevailing view of all the Allied governments, during and immediately after the war, was that Germany must be permanently controlled and made to pay for its war-mongering by massive reparations. Even though the historical precedents pointed firmly to the futility of such a solution, it was some time before the punitive approach was finally abandoned, and then only in the face of terrible social deprivation which swept across what was left of Germany in the winter of 1946–7.

Once hostilities ceased the first concern of the Soviet, the United States, the French and the United Kingdom governments seemed to be to ensure that they surrendered as little as possible of the territory conquered by their armies in the preceding six years. A treaty was out of the question since the government of the Third Reich no longer existed. Direct rule by the four major victorious powers appeared to be the only answer. Their first decision was to abolish the 1936 Anschluss agreement, combining Austria and Germany into one country. Each was separately divided into four parts, the areas roughly corresponding to the entrenched positions of the four armies. Berlin, although it was in the Soviet zone, was treated as a special case and administered jointly (Figure 6). Initially the arrangement was viewed only as a temporary administrative expedient, but the growing tension between the western Allies and the Soviet Union soon endowed it with a degree of permanence that effectively excluded the possibility of creating a single, united Germany in the years after the war. In contrast, the rapidity with which a semblance of political normality could have been restored was shown by developments in Italy. Here, since only two of the victors, the United States and the United Kingdom, were involved there was but a brief period of direct rule. In 1946, after a plebiscite, the country was allowed to return to independent democratic government. Trieste alone was not included

Figure 6   The post-war division of Germany by the occupying powers

in the agreement and remained under joint control until 1955, when it was handed over to Italy and Yugoslavia to resolve between themselves and, in so doing, created a wrangle which took twenty years to finally settle.

Part of the difficulty in securing agreement over the fate of Germany stemmed from the differing territorial ambitions of the

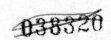

Allies. For the United Kingdom, France and the United States there was no question of making any major adjustment to frontiers; the only change of any significance was to hand over the Saar to France. For the Soviet Union, on the other hand, the end of the war and the assumption of direct rule provided a long-awaited opportunity to completely redraw the map of eastern Europe. On the Baltic coast, Estonia, Latvia and Lithuania were all permanently annexed, along with the easternmost provinces of Poland, Czechoslovakia and Rumania. Altogether the Soviet Union increased its area by more than 500,000 square kilometres and gained both partial control of the mouth of the Danube and a common frontier with Hungary, in addition to its new lands (Figure 7). It was an immeasurably stronger territorial position from which to dominate and control events in eastern Europe.

It would be wrong to give the impression that Poland, Czechoslovakia and Rumania were simply losers in this territorial reshuffle. When Poland's western frontier was pushed west to the Oder–Neisse line, it gained most of what had been the three easternmost provinces of the Third Reich, Pomerania, Brandenburg and Silesia, as well as

Figure 7   Political boundaries in Europe after 1948

the former enclave of East Prussia. Rumania was able to reclaim Transylvania in the northwest of the country, which had been occupied by Hungary between 1940 and 1944. In Czechoslovakia the effects of the 1938 Munich agreement were finally undone and, with the small exception of Ruthenia in the east, which was claimed by the Soviet Union, the 1919 boundaries agreed at the Treaty of Versailles were restored.

To redraw the frontiers of Europe boldly was one thing, but to administer the new units once they were created was quite another. Under ideal conditions it would have been difficult for foreigners to assume control; in the social, economic and political chaos of 1945, it was a monumental undertaking. Without exception the Allies saw their first task as one of subduing Germany and ensuring that the nation's industrial power was permanently curbed. None of them seem to have had any real conception of the extent of the destruction wrought on the fabric of society in the course of the six years' fighting. As a priority, they all set about preparing detailed plans for dismantling industrial machinery and plant and extorting reparations, seemingly unaware of the enormity of the social and economic problems facing the beleaguered remains of the Third Reich. The zeal with which they pursued their dismantling programmes varied considerably: the Russians were the most ruthlessly devastating and their efforts continued the longest, while the Americans were the least enthusiastic. In the British zone, which contained the whole of the Ruhr industrial area, a list of the major factories was drawn up, with a view to removing systematically the bulk of their plant. The main thrust was directed against the iron and steel and heavy engineering industries, but since all manufacturing is deeply dependent upon these basic providers, it followed inevitably that the impact of the programme would eventually permeate virtually all branches of the economy.

In practice the effects of dismantling were far less drastic than had been planned, for organizing such a massive operation was a slow and tedious business and it was strongly opposed by the Germans. They argued that it was short-sighted to continue the waste of war in peacetime and claimed that, psychologically, it could only add to the difficulties of administering the country. As a final comment, it was also pointed out that immobilizing industry would even further reduce the country's capacity to pay reparations. Despite these objections dismantling did go ahead. In the British zone, for instance, the Bochumer Verein, one of the largest iron and steel works in the Ruhr, estimated that DM 83 million worth of machinery was removed before

the policy was discontinued in 1947.[8] Such figures must, however, be
kept in perspective, for compared with the losses sustained as a result
of the wartime air offensive they were small indeed. Between 1939 and
1945 bombing caused the Bochumer Verein at least DM 280 million
worth of damage, and such proportions were typical for most of the
major firms in the Ruhr conurbation. The effects of the dismantling
programme were in fact negative in every respect, since they only
slowed down the progress towards restoring normal economic life in
Germany itself and the machinery proved, ultimately to be of little use
to the Allies, except as scrap.

The relative ineffectiveness and irrelevance of punitive measures
was illustrated in many other ways as well, one of the most blatant
being the whole question of denazification and the restoration of civil
government. In the British zone great pains were taken to establish a
new system of local government, completely free of any Nazi associa-
tions. As early as the summer of 1945 liaison committees were
appointed to act as intermediaries between the occupying forces and
the local population and, by the end of the year, all the towns in the
zone had their own elected councils. The object was to create a system
of local government, similar to that operating in Britain: the number
of paid officials was reduced and the whole system was run by
democratically elected representatives, instead of fulltime civil
servants. Unfortunately these new bodies were mostly little more than
official public contacts with the occupying forces, rather than the key
link between them and the population as a whole. Their most
important task was to identify all known Nazis, so that they could be
purged from public life, but this proved very difficult, since membership of the party had been so widespread. In practice the new bodies
fell between two stools, enjoying the confidence of neither the occupying forces or the local population.

In the last analysis, however, the most serious stumbling block to
the Allied plans for changing society was inflation. The value of the
Reichmark was reduced to nothing in the eighteen months after the
surrender and, as a result, trade and commerce came to an almost
complete standstill. The western Allies began to realize how self-
defeating their punitive measures were proving to be and they saw
that unless something was done quickly to help Germany there would
be a major social disaster. Lord Beveridge, who made a tour of the
British zone in the summer of 1946 reported that:

> There is at the moment in practically every town in the British zone (and
> it is largely an urban zone) desperate material want; deficiency of all
> the necessaries of healthy life, and almost total absence of all its com-

forts. This is not an overstatement and it is not open to question . . . The whole policy of destroying buildings and machinery on the grounds that they are war potential needs reconsideration. As for total war, everything is war potential, so that nearly everything that has war potential has peace potential and can be used to meet peace-time needs.[9]

To recreate a viable political and economic system in Germany required agreement among the four occupying powers, and it proved very difficult for the western Allies to find any common ground with the Soviet Union. The Russians' intransigent attitude was the result of a number of factors, the most important of which was an unshakable determination to see Germany permanently divided. They opposed any moves to create a single political and economic unit to replace the Third Reich for fear of a resurgence of German militarism. In fairness it must be admitted that the deprivation in the Soviet zone was rather less than in the more urbanized west, so that they were in any case under less pressure to change their initial policies. The east was generally more rural than the west and, by and large, the population was able to eke some kind of meagre existence. The smaller number of towns also meant smaller numbers of refugees flocking into them, thus further reducing the overall scale of deprivation in the Soviet zone.

There was great reluctance on the part of the western Allies to take dramatic unilateral action to revitalize the German economy and political system. It was realized that such a split would almost certainly cause a serious quarrel with the Soviet Union. Not only was this undesirable for its own sake but at this time also there was a large measure of public sympathy in the west for the aims of Russian policy in Germany, especially when the extent to which the Soviet Union had been devastated in the war itself became more generally known. The Communist Party and its ideology enjoyed widespread popular support in Europe, but this enthusiasm began to wane rapidly as the ruthless tactics it was prepared to use to gain power became more obvious.

In Soviet-occupied eastern Europe the Communist takeover was not immediate, but it was sure and thorough. Each national communist party prepared its own plans for securing permanent control of the party machine, beginning with Bulgaria in 1945 and then spreading to Poland, Czechoslovakia, Rumania and Hungary. In Yugoslavia and Albania the process was already complete before the end of the Second World War, since Communist partisans had successfully organized the resistance to the German occupation in both countries. The relatively leisurely progress of the Communist takeover in those east European countries where they were not already in power when the war ended underlined two important points about the diffusion of Communism after 1945. First, although the national parties enjoyed Soviet help and encouragement, it is now clear that they were operating much more independently than was believed at the time in the west. Secondly, although they had a measure of public support, nowhere were they initially the majority party and, in consequence, they had to proceed somewhat cautiously in taking over the levers of political power. Nevertheless, by 1948 not only was each of the eight countries, which now form eastern Europe, under Communist control, they were all dominated by the Soviet Union. The Cominform was set up in that year to co-ordinate the efforts of the various national party organizations and, based in Moscow, it quickly became the chief medium for Soviet control. Only Yugoslavia attempted to resist Russian domination, and one of the main sanctions it had to suffer was expulsion from the Cominform in 1948. In addition to such political reprisals, the Soviet Union was in a doubly strong position to dictate the pattern of events, because its troops remained stationed throughout eastern Europe after 1945.

Attempted Communist takeovers were not confined to Soviet-occupied territories and it was developments in western Europe which really awakened public opinion in the western Allied countries to the seriousness and ruthlessness of Communist intentions. The vicious though short-lived attempts at revolution in Belgium, Greece and Turkey opened the flood-gates to massive, direct American intervention in post-war European affairs to counter Communist infiltration. First of all President Truman pledged the support of the United States to any country threatened by Communist military pressure and, in 1947, $400 million worth of aid was put at the disposal of Greece and Turkey to combat the threat. A second and, in the long-term, more significant development was the signing of a collective defence agreement, the Brussels Treaty, on 17 March 1948, by the United Kingdom, France and the Benelux countries. It was warmly welcomed by the United States and was the first concrete step by the countries of western Europe to form a common front against the threat of Soviet aggression.

All these developments had a direct impact on the future of Germany. By 1948 it was obvious that the *de facto* division of the country by the Iron Curtain would become a more or less permanent feature, for it was clear that the Soviet Union and the other Allies would never be able to come to any agreement. In the Soviet zone the Communist Party had been gradually installed in control, despite receiving very little support at the polls, and in 1950 the Russians recognized the German Democratic Republic as a separate Communist state. In the British, French and American zones the economic revival was well underway and the three occupying powers decided to proceed jointly with a separate political solution. In 1954 the three zones were merged, under the terms of the Paris Treaty, to form the Federal Republic of Germany, thus giving formal recognition to a political division which had already existed for six years.

Any reservations in the west about the advisability of unilateral action over Germany were finally dispelled by the Berlin blockade. Berlin, the former capital of the Third Reich, although isolated from the west in the middle of the Soviet zone, was nevertheless administered jointly. There had always been some difficulty in maintaining road and rail access, but on 24 June 1948 the Russians closed all land approaches to the city and tried to starve out the Allies. Only a daring and massive airlift of supplies from western Europe saved the situation and kept the beleaguered city open. It was an incredible and unique operation involving daily flights and the transfer of thousands of tons of food and all other raw materials. The blockade lasted for more than a year, until 12 May 1949, and by the time it was lifted the Soviet bluff had been called and the countries of western Europe had cast their lot firmly with the United States. Any immediate thought of a united Germany embracing both east and west had been abandoned.

3

The Atlantic Community and European Integration

The American View of Europe

In retrospect it is apparent that there was little or no chance of the European states containing and neutralizing the competing ambitions of the United States and the Soviet Union in the years immediately after the end of the Second World War. Whatever the rights and wrongs of the respective cases of the two super-powers, the conflict had brought them face to face and political institutions had to begin to take account of that fact.

In western Europe two organizations, the Organization for European Economic Co-operation (OEEC) and the North Atlantic Treaty Organization (NATO), both primarily the product of American thinking, firmly stamped the imprint of the United States on the European scene. The OEEC was concerned with economic relations between the west European states; NATO was responsible for defence and collective security. Together they dominated the whole pattern of political integration in the years after 1945.

The two organizations forced west European nations to look for more permanent ties within an Atlantic rather than a purely European community, thus formalizing a tendency that had been gathering ground throughout the twentieth century. However, the OEEC and NATO also encouraged a revaluation of internal relationships. The American view of Europe at that time was markedly different from that of the majority of Europeans. The citizens of so manifestly a successful union as the United States found it hard to comprehend the resistance and even hostility that the whole concept of integration and co-operation generated on the other side of the Atlantic. The mystique surrounding the individuality and independence of the small

34

nation state was something towards which Americans were frankly unsympathetic; they viewed it as a curious anachronism, unrelated to the needs and realities of the second half of the twentieth century. Their general attitude is reflected in the story of an American business-man flying to Europe, who, on being informed that he was now over France, snapped back that he did not want to be bothered with details![1] This impatience with small-scale nationalism also struck a chord with many European politicians in the wake of a world war; certainly it gave encouragement to the incipient movements striving for a greater measure of political and economic integration. There can be little doubt that but for the continuing involvement of the United States in west European affairs the multi-national ideals and aspira-tions, fostered and developed during the past thirty years, would have made much slower headway.

The Organization for European Economic Co-operation

The cornerstone of western Europe's economic revival was the OEEC. Its aim was 'the achievement of a sound European economy through the economic co-operation of its members'[2] and, as Elkin has pointed out, the use of the word 'economy' in the singular is significant and certainly no accident.[3] The Convention for European Economic Co-operation was signed on 16 April 1948 by Austria, Belgium, Denmark, France, Greece, Iceland, Eire, Italy, Luxembourg, the Netherlands, Norway, Portugal, Sweden, Switzerland, Turkey and the United Kingdom, together with the commanders-in-chief of the British, French and United States occupation zones in Germany (Figure 8). Subsequently, in 1949, the Federal Republic of Germany became a full member in its own right, taking over from the commanders-in-chief of the Zones of Occupation on the Council. In 1950 both Canada and the United States accepted invitations to become associate members of the OEEC, entitling them to co-operate on an unofficial basis in matters of common interest. There were few further changes in the organization. In 1955 Spain was permitted to participate fully in the Ministerial Committee for Agriculture and Food, the Committee of Deputies and their sub-committees, but not in the full Council, and, in the same year, Yugoslavia was allowed to attend technical committees and sub-committees as an observer. In 1959 Spain finally became a full member. The main achievement of the OEEC was the creation and maintenance of a liberalized trading and currency system between the member nations, for this was to be the foundation of European prosperity in the 1950s and 1960s.

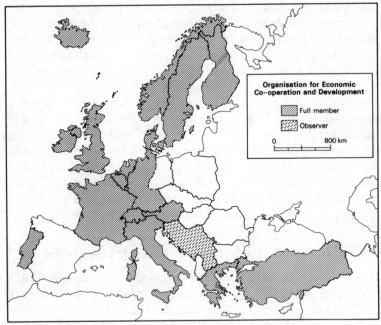

Figure 8   Membership of the Organization for Economic Co-operation and Development 1977

In many ways, however, the OEEC was an afterthought, foisted onto Europe at the insistence of the United States as the price of American economic aid. In 1945, once military victory had been achieved, there was a strong and widely held view in the United States that its obligations to Europe were at an end and that both military and economic aid should be rapidly phased out. During the war itself, under the terms of the lend-lease programme, billions of dollars had been distributed amongst the European allies to bolster their economies and the United States was now looking for repayment of these loans rather than renewals. That most of the indebted European nations would have had to bankrupt themselves to repay the money seems to have been a fact almost totally lost on the government in Washington. In economic terms America's former allies, France and the United Kingdom, had suffered almost as severely as the conquered Germany and Italy and they both desperately needed further advances in the immediate post-war period. Indeed their problems were exacerbated, because the funds of the United Nations Relief and Rehabilitation Administration, set up in advance of the United Nations proper to distribute relief aid, were only available under the most stringent conditions. Ironically, both the United Kingdom and France found themselves effectively barred from making claims, despite their being in a perilous economic plight, because investments in overseas territories were counted as part of their overall assets, even though there was not the slightest chance of their being realized to help alleviate the short-term problems.

The impasse continued for well over a year, but by 1947 the seriousness of the economic crisis in Europe and its implications for United States trade and security were beginning to dawn on the Americans. A gradual reversal of policy took place, culminating in a decision to mount a massive aid programme, aimed at putting the European economy back on a firm footing. The chief architect of the European Recovery Programme was the then US Secretary of State, George C. Marshall, which led to it being almost universally referred to at the time as the 'Marshall Plan'. The main objective was to encourage industrial reconstruction and the bulk of the aid was in the form of food and raw materials, rather than finished products. This was thought to be the best way of stimulating both manufacturing and employment in Europe, since the local economies would have to become involved in the actual preparation of materials for the consumer market and not merely be responsible for distribution. The bulk of the programme spanned the period from 1948 to 1952 and involved the equivalent of $13,500 million. The United Kingdom received the largest share ($3,176 million), but France ($2,706 million), Italy ($1,474 million) and West Germany ($1,389 million) were also allocated substantial sums.

One of the few conditions attached to aid under the Marshall Plan was that the participating countries should accept a common programme of recovery and that they should establish a permanent organization for achieving this end. France and the United Kingdom took the lead in satisfying this condition and invited all European countries to a conference in Paris in 1947. Unfortunately the schism between the Communist and the non-Communist governments emerged all too clearly and the only western countries to accept were those who subsequently became full members of the OEEC. Despite the overt opposition of the Soviet Union and the Communist governments of eastern Europe, it was decided to proceed with the creation of a permanent organization. However, it was made quite clear that membership could be extended at any time to include other European countries.

The outcome was far removed from what the Americans had originally envisaged. Marshall had made it quite clear initially that he intended the European Recovery Programme to include the whole of Europe and not just the western nations. He was as keen as any European to remain on good terms with the Soviet Union, not least because he realized that the United States would have to step into any breach that developed. In the event, not only did the Soviet Union and the east European states refuse to have anything to do with the proposals, they labelled them as 'a plan to subjugate Europe' and made it quite clear that, in their view, the whole scheme was nothing more than a bare-faced attempt to consolidate United States' political influence through economic aid.[4] From the point of view of western Europe, the European Recovery Programme was one of the most generous and decisive economic actions of the century, but without question it precipitated precisely the political polarization the United States had sought to avoid. It was instrumental in formally crystallizing the map of Europe into two blocs, divided by the Iron Curtain.

Once the OEEC had been set up, its first task was to decide how Marshall Aid was to be divided between the member states. It was an exceptionally difficult assignment, but agreement was finally reached and it marked a decisive step forward on the road towards peacetime co-operation in Europe. The method was simple and direct: a steering committee, comprising the United Kingdom, France, Italy and the Netherlands, was given the task of devising tentative allocations; their proposals were then presented to a full meeting of all member nations, who, after appropriate revisions, eventually accepted a modified version. For the final three years of the European Recovery Programme the system was simplified even further. A special committee, comprising the Chairman of the Council and the Secretary General, was appointed to arbitrate on the original steering committee allocations, thus bypassing the general debate completely. The manner in which agreement was reached, using a peer group to put forward initial proposals, was to be a model for future co-operative ventures in Europe and was one of the first signs of any willingness to relinquish national sovereignty over economic decision-making.

Distributing Marshall Aid was a crucial part of the OEEC's early work and was the main reason for the establishment of the organization in the first place, but it was only a relatively minor feature of the fundamental long-term aims, as set out in the Convention. Under the general exhortation to create a sound European economy, the members set themselves a whole series of economic, financial and commercial objectives. They pledged themselves to expand production by using resources and manpower as efficiently and effectively as possible. Full employment and free movement of labour within the member countries were seen as essential prerequisites of this policy and the organization took steps to achieve both. Among other things, the European Productivity Agency was set up; steps were taken to co-ordinate large-scale investment projects in member countries; and, to guard against times of scarcity, procedures were worked out for allocating raw materials and ensuring that they were used as judiciously as possible.

The general expansion of trade and the removal of all restrictions to the free movement of goods and capital were also seen as being essential to continuing and soundly based economic growth. Member countries were encouraged to abolish both quantitative restrictions on imports, export controls and government aids to exports. The OEEC itself also sought to find ways and means of reducing restrictions on the movement of capital and this led directly to the creation of the European Payments Union (see below, page 41).

The Convention also called on members to look at the possibilities for strengthening their economic links by a greater measure of economic integration. In this way the OEEC gave powerful encouragement to other movements, leading eventually to the creation of the European Economic Community and the European Free Trade Association. Finally each member was committed to preserving and, if possible, enhancing its domestic economic position. This was of crucial importance because it was only possible for the free market to work properly if there was a fairly high level of stability between the constituent economies.

The structure of the organization seeking to implement these varied and far-reaching economic aims was extremely simple (Figure 9). The supreme authority was the Council, consisting of representatives of all the member and associate member governments. It had ultimate control over all operations and decisions, although it was assisted in its day-to-day work by an Executive Committee. The seven members of the Executive Committee were appointed annually from among the leaders of the national delegations to the full Council and their job was to filter the mass of business coming before the Council itself, so as to produce a workable agenda. The Executive Committee was in turn serviced by a permanent staff under the direction of the Secretary General. The Council remained permanently in session and was therefore able to function continuously, although the level of representation varied according to the importance of the matters under discussion.

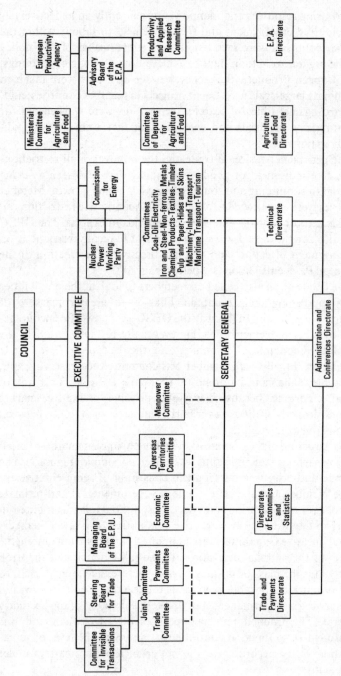

Figure 9   The organizational structure of the Organization for European Economic Co-operation

Voting in the OEEC Council followed the 'unanimity rule', which required the support of all members before any decision could be ratified. There were a few exceptions: a member could exclude itself voluntarily, if not directly affected by a particular proposal; and the Council could exclude a member of its own accord, if that member had ceased to fulfil its obligations under the Convention. Nevertheless, in general the unanimity rule prevailed. Once a decision had been taken it was binding on all members, but implementation was a matter for the individual countries; the organization had neither the power nor the resources to force compliance by direct action. This point is important when comparing the OEEC with later organizations, such as the European Economic Community, where direct action is possible and certain aspects of national sovereignty compromised. In the OEEC, however, such a possibility was recognized and specifically guarded against by making all implementation the responsibility of individual member governments.

In certain areas, notably the liberalization of trade, the system worked well. Each country went ahead on its own and progressively reduced import controls and subsidies for exports, and generally went a long way towards creating conditions of completely free movement for industrial products within the OEEC. In other respects, however, the lack of centralized powers for direct action was less satisfactory and as time went on and the organization developed it was compelled to assume a number of operational activities.

The most important of these was the European Payments Union (EPU) set up in 1950. The aim of the EPU was to make the settlement of monetary transactions between member countries quick and easy, so that trade might not be inhibited by problems of convertibility among the different currencies. Payments were undertaken on a monthly basis, with all other currency areas taken as a group and the net positions settled by a combination of credits and gold payments. Any deficit which exceeded a country's agreed credit had to be settled entirely in gold. Although the EPU had no independent legal status and derived all its authority through the Council of the OEEC, the members gave the Managing Board the power to require compliance with its decisions on credit management. The arrangement was a tremendous advance on the complicated system of bilateral agreements which it replaced. Elkin has estimated that there were more than four hundred of these operating between European countries and between them and the outside world in 1954.[5] Most were gradually subsumed into the single multilateral EPU system between 1950 and 1958, thus avoiding the situation where a country in deficit with its partner country was unable to use its surplus with a third country to off-set the debt.

By the late 1950s, however, it was becoming clear that a system that had made the European currencies transferable among themselves was not, on its own, a sufficient basis for keeping the system of free trade operating in the wider Atlantic community. In 1958, therefore, it was replaced by the European Monetary Agreement, which, like the EPU, was part of the OEEC, but sought to encompass a much wider brief. Under the European Monetary Agreement monthly settlements were made without recourse to credit, emphasizing the immeasurably stronger economic circumstances of all European states, and its scope was extended beyond Europe to include all those countries in the sterling and French franc areas. Since convertability with the US dollar was also achieved for most OEEC countries in 1958, the European Monetary Agreement represented a very considerable extension of the multilateral ideal embodied in the former EPU.

The other operational activities of the OEEC were less fundamental and direct in their impact on the relationships between the nations of western Europe. The European Productivity Agency, which was created in 1953, was primarily envisaged as a body to stimulate and co-ordinate ways and means of improving productivity in each individual country. The methods employed depended largely on the particular problems of the various members of the OEEC and, in practice, most of the work of the European Productivity Agency involved facilitating the exchange of information through publication, exchanges of personnel and international seminars and meetings. In particular it was concerned with promoting the transfer of American techniques and methods to Europe. Without doubt it performed a useful co-ordinating role but it is extremely difficult to gauge its precise impact because of the purely advisory nature of its brief.

The European Nuclear Energy Agency was the final operational achievement of the OEEC. Set up formally at the end of 1957, its purpose was to co-ordinate research and development by member countries into the peaceful uses of nuclear energy. The agency was created against a background of general concern, especially on the part of the French, about future sources of energy. In the mid-1950s nuclear energy seemed to be the most promising option, although in the course of events development has taken much longer than expected and oil has subsequently emerged as the major source of industrial fuel. As a result the European Nuclear Energy Agency and Euratom, with which it was closely linked, have so far played a relatively minor role in the work of the OEEC and the European Community respectively. Nevertheless, research into ways of producing nuclear energy more efficiently has continued since the late 1950s in various European countries, especially Norway and the United Kingdom. So far the results have been solid rather than spectacular but the recent political militancy of many oil-producing countries and the rapidly rising cost of crude oil have reawakened interest in nuclear energy as a source of fuel and attempts have been made to enhance the status of the European Nuclear Energy Agency.

Many of the achievements of the OEEC in the 1950s were far in advance of those by more overtly supranational organizations, such as the European Economic Community, more than a decade later. The EPU and the European Monetary Agreement were among the first effective developments in the field of international economic and monetary control and, together with the removal of restrictions on the movement of goods, they were the basis of the post-war economic recovery in Europe. Figure 10 shows clearly the sustained general

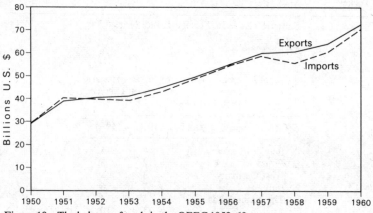

Figure 10   The balance of trade in the OEEC 1950–60

improvement in trade between 1950 and 1960. The volume of trade more than doubled in real terms over the decade and in the OEEC as a whole there was a healthy surplus of exports over imports, especially after 1958.

It is, however, somewhat misleading to look at the OEEC as a single trading entity. As an international organization it derived its strength from the success of its individual members, and not all of them prospered equally during this period. In absolute terms all

Table 1 THE GROWTH OF EXPORTS IN REAL TERMS IN THE OEEC 1950–1960

	Total exports 1950 ($US 1000)	Total exports 1960 at 1950 prices $US 1000	% increase or decrease in total exports at 1950 prices
Belgium/Luxembourg	2,633,451	3,407,433	29
France	4,068,667	4,529,333	11
West Germany	3,471,034	9,816,734	182
Italy	1,629,284	3,082,014	89
The Netherlands	1,926,701	3,141,640	63
Austria	453,824	929,890	104
Denmark	836,914	1,170,270	40
Norway	619,271	694,877	12
Portugal	262,906	301,050	15
Sweden	1,780,762	1,949,114	9
Switzerland	1,088,371	1,721,556	58
United Kingdom	7,212,054	7,822,227	8
Greece	101,747	130,053	27
Iceland	44,523	43,877	−1·5
Eire	232,462	344,488	48
Turkey	313,688	83,313	−74·3

Source: OECD Statistical Bulletin, Foreign Trade, Series C.

Table 2 RANK ORDER OF OEEC MEMBER COUNTRIES BY VALUE OF EXPORTS, 1950 AND 1960

	1950	1960
Belgium/Luxembourg	4	5
France	2	3
West Germany	3	1
Italy	7	6
The Netherlands	5	4
Austria	11	10
Denmark	9	9
Norway	10	11
Portugal	13	13
Sweden	6	7
Switzerland	8	8
United Kingdom	1	2
Greece	15	15
Iceland	16	16
Eire	14	12
Turkey	12	14

Table 3 INTRA OEEC EXPORTS 1950 AND 1960

	Exports to other OEEC countries 1950 ($US 1000)	% of total	Exports to other OEFC countries 1960 ($US 1000)	% of total
Belgium/Luxembourg	1,601,790	61	2,596,744	68
France	1,434,493	35	3,199,825	46
West Germany	2,159,820	62	6,920,930	61
Italy	838,070	51	1,982,512	54
The Netherlands	1,221,086	63	2,818,653	70
Austria	287,593	63	730,304	65
Denmark	645,923	77	1,073,015	73
Norway	385,630	62	627,402	71
Portugal	113,840	43	143,904	44
Sweden	1,112,046	62	1,750,162	68
Switzerland	536,564	49	1,110,487	59
United Kingdom	1,904,507	26	3,008,263	30
Greece	73,721	72	99,048	49
Iceland	26,186	59	34,493	52
Eire	207,015	89	342,117	83
Turkey	181,407	58	173,592	54

Source: OECD Statistical Bulletin, Foreign Trade, Series C.

sixteen countries (Spain is excluded from the subsequent analysis, since it only became a full member in 1959) enjoyed a sharp increase in the value of their trade between 1950 and 1960, even though at constant prices the improvement was much less dramatic. As can be seen from Table 1, West Germany and Austria were able to more than double the value of exports in real terms over the period, although, in both cases, their economies started from an extremely low point as a result of the war. Italy, the Netherlands and Switzerland all achieved increases in excess of 50 per cent, and of the rest Belgium, Luxembourg, France, Denmark, Norway, Portugal, Sweden, the United Kingdom, Greece and Eire experienced more modest improvements. There is no real pattern to the variations. Some of the largest industrial producers, such as France and the United Kingdom, were only moderately successful in increasing the overall level of their exports, while others, in particular the Benelux countries, saw a dramatic upturn in their fortunes. There was just as little consistency amongst the smaller, less industrialized countries. Eire, Switzerland and Denmark all sharply increased the volume of their exports, but other countries, including Norway, Portugal, Iceland and Turkey, found it much harder to share in the general rise in prosperity. Despite these variations, there were few really significant changes in the relative positions of the individual countries in the OEEC in terms of their importance as exporters. As can be seen from Table 2, West Germany overtook both France and the United Kingdom to rise from third place in 1950 to first in 1960, but for the rest the relative changes only involved a movement of one place either up or down the league table. In other words, the growth trade in the OEEC between 1950 and 1960 did not fundamentally alter the balance of industrial power between the individual states.

As far as each member was concerned, it was the overall increase in its level of trade which was important, but for the OEEC itself the degree to which any increase was diverted to the west European market was also a matter of considerable secondary importance. Table 3 shows clearly that among the larger industrial countries there was a sharp increase in the level of intra-European trade. In addition to the increase in the value of exports, there was also a significant rise in the proportion of trade concentrated within western Europe between 1950 and 1960. The most extreme case was that of Switzerland. In 1950 it sold $US 536,564,000 worth of goods to other members of the OEEC, 49 per cent of its total exports, but by 1960 the gross figure had risen to $US 1,110,487,000 and accounted for 59 per cent of Switzerland's total exports. The only major industrial country where the proportion actually fell was West Germany, but in this case the general increase in its level of exports was such that it too experienced a sharp rise in real terms in the value of its European trade. One interesting point to emerge from Table 3 is the relative lack of success of the smaller members of the OEEC in raising the proportion of their exports which went to other member countries. Denmark, Greece, Iceland, Eire and Turkey all suffered a relative decline and, in the case of Greece, the fall was quite a steep one.

One feature of the structure of trade in the OEEC which was to have important repercussions for the future pattern of European integration was the relatively small proportion of the United Kingdom's exports which went to Europe. In 1950 only 26 per cent were sold to other members of the OEEC, and by 1960 the proportion had only risen to 30 per cent, in both cases very much lower than any other member country. This lack of economic involvement in Europe goes a long way towards explaining the United Kingdom's muted enthusiasm for European political and economic union in the 1950s and 1960s. It is significant too to compare this situation with that in France. In 1950 France sent nearly two-thirds of its exports outside Europe, but by 1960 the proportion was only just over half. After the Second World War France and the United Kingdom were the European states with the largest overseas dependencies, but in the

1950s France withdrew from most of these commitments and turned increasingly towards its European neighbours. In the United Kingdom this process did not really gather momentum until after 1960 and, as a result, the United Kingdom government did not participate as fully as it might have done in the economic restructuring of western Europe.

The main achievement of the OEEC was to convince the countries of western Europe that their future lay in mutual co-operation, rather than factional hostility. By itself this would have been a major contribution, but the OEEC went further and devised mechanisms, such as the EPU, which translated the ideal into hard economic fact. The effect has been to change fundamentally the structure of political and economic relations not only in Europe but in much of the rest of the world as well.

The Organization for Economic Co-operation and Development

By 1958 it was becoming clear that many of the original objectives of the OEEC had been achieved and there was widespread doubt as to whether a purely European framework was the most suitable one for ensuring continued economic prosperity. Within Europe, a liberalized trading system and free currency convertibility were facts and it was clear that there were insuperable political objections to the OEEC's other long-term aim, a free trade area comprising all west European countries.

The standing of western Europe in world terms had radically altered in the decade since 1948. Post-war reconstruction had been successfully completed and no longer was it possible or, from a European point of view, even desirable for the United States to treat western Europe as an ailing relative. There was considerable disquiet about the extent of United States economic involvement and, in 1967, J. J. Servan-Schreiber published a polemic entitled 'Le défi américain'[6] in which he estimated that the Americans had invested over $US 14 billion in western Europe, $US 10 billion since 1958. He called on all Europeans to throw off the yoke of American economic imperialism, especially in the form of multi-national companies. In many ways the message was remarkably similar to that embodied in the Soviet rejection of Marshall Aid twenty years previously. Clearly western Europe and North America had now to co-operate on a more equal basis, and the arguments for an Atlantic, rather than a European organization were overwhelming. The developing countries required assistance from all those sections of the industrialized world in a position to provide it. A joint approach to development aid was needed, involving not only Europe and North America, but other industrialized countries as well. Many of the OEEC institutions were also out of date. The replacement of the EPU by the European Monetary Agreement and the fact that European currencies were now internationally convertible made a purely European payments system unnecessary and irrelevant, as were unilateral measures to liberalize trade. These functions could be handled more appropriately by the International Monetary Fund[7] and the General Agreement on Tariffs and Trade[8] respectively. Equally the much improved interchange of technical information meant that the European Productivity Agency had also largely outlived its usefulness.

In 1960 a small group was appointed by the Council of the OEEC to look into all these problems and, as a direct result of its deliberations, the organization was wound up and replaced by the Organization for Economic Co-operation and Development (OECD) under the terms of a convention signed in December 1960, coming into force on 30 September 1961. Although the OECD grew out of the OEEC, the scope of the new organization was much greater, reflecting the changed political and economic circumstances. The United States and Canada were full founder members and its significance was extended beyond Europe and the Atlantic when Japan became a member in 1964, Finland in 1969 and Australia in 1971. In addition, Yugoslavia participates fully in many of the economic discussions and has observer status for most others, and New Zealand is a full member of the Committee for Agriculture. Kristensen succinctly summed up the character of the membership when he described it as being in economic terms the organization of the industrialized countries with market economies.[9]

The basic functions of the OECD derive from a central desire to promote economic growth and the expansion of world trade. The concept is similar to that of the OEEC but there is a clear-cut shift away from internal economic reconstruction towards concern for developing nations. The organization sees sustained economic growth in industrialized countries as the best way of providing capital for developing countries. The Development Assistance Committee and the Development Centre have formed the cornerstones of OECD's operations and there has been close co-operation with other development agencies, especially those established under the auspices of the United Nations.

One of the most notable features of the OECD is the broad view it has taken of economic growth. Economic trends in all the member countries have been continuously and rigorously monitored, not just for their own sake, but also because of the organization's belief in the crucial importance of an economically healthy industrialized world for the developing world as a whole. Care has also been taken to foster education and research, it being argued strongly that economic growth and development can only flourish if manpower resources are used to the full and new knowledge is actively sought. Similarly the causes of environmental protection and pollution have been vigorously pursued, because they are seen as being symptomatic of potential waste in the economic system.

The OECD is a very wide-ranging organization working in a global rather than a European context. Whereas the OEEC was fundamental to the whole process of European integration, the OECD is more an expression of the economic self-confidence built up during the 1950s. It is hard to imagine the OECD existing independently of the moves towards economic integration in Europe, but the organization itself has made little direct contribution to those developments.

North Atlantic Treaty Organization

The military corollary of the OEEC is the North Atlantic Treaty Organization (NATO), which came into being on 4 April 1949 and has functioned with relatively small modifications ever since (Figure 11). The organization has evoked pungent criticism from non-members, notably the Soviet Union, for the belligerent undertones of its treaty of incorporation, but this has been compensated for by the extravagant praise from its apologists. The latter claim that since the treaty was signed the spread of Communism in Europe has been effectively contained, pointing out that not a single European nation has been lost to Communist aggression. It is also claimed that without the security of the NATO deterrent, the upsurge in economic prosperity and the rapid progress towards economic and political unity in western Europe would have been very much slowed down. It is almost impossible to substantiate such claims now, one way or the other, but there is absolutely no doubt about the influence of NATO in shaping the future of post-war western Europe, not least because of the financial commitment it entailed. As can be seen from Table 4, the proportion of the combined Gross National Products of the European members of the alliance spent on defence was never less than 5 per cent between 1950 and 1970 and, in 1952, rose as high as 8.7 per cent. The bulk of this expenditure was devoted to the defence of Europe and, therefore, pumped directly into the European economy.

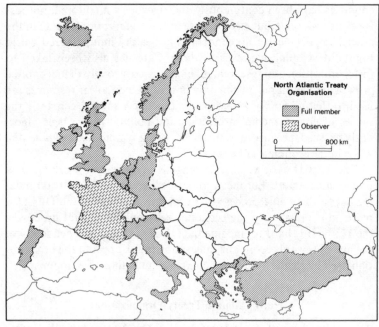

Figure 11   Membership of the North Atlantic Treaty Organization 1977

The need for a north Atlantic defence organization was not immediately apparent after 1945. In the first flush of enthusiasm after the signing of the United Nations charter, it appeared that this body would be able to provide sufficiently strong guarantees against military aggression. However such hopes were quickly dashed in Europe. No attempt was made to reduce the numbers of Russian troops in Europe after the war had ended, and the major west European nations were deeply concerned at the ease with which Communist governments were established in Poland, Czechoslovakia, Bulgaria, Rumania and Hungary (see above, page 32), while the United Nations looked on, apparently powerless.

Gradually these concerns were translated into action. In 1947 the United States Congress accepted the Truman Doctrine, pledging American support for all free peoples resisting subjugation by armed minorities or outside pressure. In particular the policy was aimed initially at Greece and Turkey, since both countries were trying to quell Communist uprisings, but its provisions were intended to be universally applicable. The potential threat also drove western Europe to unilateral action and, in 1948, representatives of Belgium, France,

Table 4 THE PROPORTION OF THE GROSS NATIONAL PRODUCTS OF NATO MEMBER COUNTRIES DEVOTED TO DEFENCE EXPENDITURE 1950– 1970

Year	European members	North American members	Total
1950	5·9	5.3	5.4
1951	7·1	10·6	9·8
1952	8·7	14·5	13·0
1953	8·0	14·4	12·4
1954	7·2	12·4	10·8
1955	6·6	10·8	9·4
1956	6·7	10·4	9·2
1957	6·4	10·5	9·2
1958	5·8	10·6	9·0
1959	6·0	9·9	8·7
1960	5·8	9·5	8·2
1961	5·7	9·6	8·3
1962	5·9	9·8	8·5
1963	5·9	9·3	8·1
1964	5·6	8·5	7·5
1965	5·4	7·9	7·0
1966	5·3	8·8	7·6
1967	5·4	9·7	8·2
1968	5·2	10·1	8·5
1969	5·3	9·8	8·0
1970	5·2	9·0	7·9

Source: NATO – facts and figures.

Luxembourg, the Netherlands and the United Kingdom met to sign a common defence treaty, guaranteeing the support of all should any one of the signatories be attacked. In fact the European concern was less with the Soviet Union than with renewed aggression by Germany and this was specifically written into the terms of the Brussels Treaty, but even at this early juncture the potential Russian threat was an important subsidiary consideration.

The effect on both the Soviet Union and the United States of the Brussels Treaty and the emergence of a common defence front in western Europe was electric, but in sharp contrast. The Russians retaliated with the Berlin blockade and an unsuccessful attempt to precipitate precisely the sort of confrontation with which the treaty was designed to cope. The Americans, on the other hand, reacted by floating the idea of a mutual defence agreement which would include the United States and Canada as well as the Europeans countries. It was a proposal warmly welcomed on both sides of the Atlantic, and NATO became an established fact in the spring of 1949. The members were the signatories to the Brussels Treaty, together with the United States and Canada and five other European countries, Denmark,

Iceland, Italy, Norway and Portugal. Subsequently the membership was enlarged to include Greece and Turkey in February 1952 and the Federal Republic of Germany in 1955.

NATO has always been first and foremost a military alliance built around the concept of collective security. The most important provision of the treaty is Article 5 which states that: 'The Parties agree that an armed attack against one or more of them in Europe or North America shall be considered an attack against them all . . .'[10] The language is blunt and unequivocal, leaving no doubt about the responsibilities it confers upon the signatories. Initially the geographical area covered by the treaty was closely defined as the territory of any of the member nations in Europe or North America, the Algerian *départements* of France and islands administered by any of the signatories north of the Tropic of Cancer. It also covered attacks on occupation forces elsewhere in Europe and attacks on ships and aircraft in the North Atlantic area. Subsequently, when Greece and Turkey became members, the area covered was extended to include Turkey, and the Mediterranean was made subject to the same provisions as the North Atlantic area. However, the purposes of the treaty are not solely military and it also provides for co-operation in political, social and economic matters. The multifunctional role is a natural extension of the fundamental thinking behind NATO: it has always been seen as a means of defending 'a way of life not only by military means but also through co-operation in political, economic, social and cultural fields'.[11]

The supreme authority of NATO is the civilian North Atlantic Council, which is in permanent session with ambassadors representing each member. Two or three times a year the Council meets at ministerial level to discuss the more important issues of policy. Under the Council there are two separate structures, one civil and the other military. The civil structure comprises an executive branch directed by the Secretary General and a series of specialist committees, dealing with such matters as political affairs, armament, economic affairs, defence review and so on. The military structure is governed by a sub-committee of the Council called the Defence Planning Committee. This civilian sub-committee controls a military committee with an international staff and three regional commands, covering the Atlantic, Europe and the Channel. There is also, in addition, a regional planning group for Canada and the United States.

There are three broad phases to the work and achievements of NATO in Europe. The first, from 1949 to about 1955, was mainly concerned with establishing an organization capable of fulfilling the considerable commitments that the treaty imposed on its members. During this period the membership was expanded (see above, page 52) and it was agreed that the cornerstone of NATO's policy should be an integrated European defence force. This was a decision taken in the wake of the Korean War. The agreement was successfully put that the only possible way to combat a European equivalent of the invasion of South Korea by the Communists was by joint planning and an integrated military command. The first Supreme Allied Commander in Europe was General Dwight D. Eisenhower, and the cohesion and co-operation which he and his successors achieved in the joint military command was an important factor in promoting more general integration in western Europe. The crowning achievement of this phase of NATO's work was the Paris Agreement, signed in 1954, formally terminating the occupation by France, Britain and United States of the Federal Republic of Germany and admitting it to full membership of the organization. This marked the consolidation of the alliance and also a degree of voluntary military integration in western Europe unprecedented in peacetime.

The second phase, from 1955 to 1964, was concerned with containing both the political and military threat of the Soviet Union, in Europe and elsewhere, and with maintaining the cohesion among the individual members. This latter task was by no means easy, as the organization had to survive several internal crises during the 1950s. The independent action of the United Kingdom and France in Suez in 1956 was a serious threat to the alliance and would almost certainly have had more far-reaching repercussions but for the invasion of Hungary by the Soviet Union in the autumn of the same year. Hungary was proof, if any further proof were needed, that there had been no relaxation in the Soviet determination to maintain and if possible extend the jurisdiction of its own particular brand of Communism. As far as western Europe was concerned it strongly reaffirmed the need for NATO and prevented any moves towards fragmentation within the organization. Throughout the latter half of the 1950s and the early 1960s the NATO members presented a more or less united front, speaking with one voice in a whole series of negotiations with the Soviet Union, aimed at defusing international tensions in Europe and controlling the spread of nuclear weapons. The alliance was instrumental in maintaining a somewhat uneasy peace, despite the growing rivalry between the United States and the Soviet Union.

The most recent phase, from 1965 onwards, has seen a marked change in the whole pattern of relationships both inside and outside

NATO. In the past decade the sharp divide between eastern and western Europe has been somewhat softened and, as a result, the organization's political objectives have become less clear and its energies somewhat diffused. A number of factors have contributed to this gradual change, but most important has been the growing tension between the Soviet Union and China. The Sino-Soviet dispute, which dragged on throughout the 1960s, made Russia aware of the undesirability of having hostile neighbours on all fronts and encouraged moves towards détente with the more amenable European countries. The industrial democracies of western Europe, in turn, were not slow to appreciate the advantages of a more relaxed political climate, and trade agreements and cultural exchanges proliferated.

Naturally there was considerable variation in the enthusiasm with which individual countries embraced the new spirit of détente, but, for some, NATO loomed as a positive impediment to any further relaxation of tension. Foremost among the doubters was France. President De Gaulle had a grand vision of a European axis linking Paris to Moscow, in place of what he saw as the Anglo-Saxon domination of west European politics. In March 1966 he withdrew all French forces from NATO, without however abandoning the alliance itself. Nevertheless, all the administrative facilities in France had to be moved: the military headquarters went to Brussels, the Defence College to Rome and the Central European Command to Brussum in the Netherlands. It was a traumatic experience which shook the military self-confidence of the other members and weakened the impact of the whole alliance. For the first time in nearly eighteen years there was an open division in the common west European defence front.

The victory of the Social Democrats at the 1970 election in the Federal Republic of Germany also caused fundamental, though less dramatic changes. The new Chancellor, Herr Brandt, was determined to pursue a more conciliatory line with Germany's eastern neighbours, and a succession of treaties and non-aggression pacts were negotiated. The culmination was a treaty with Russia, signed in 1972, which accepted the existing *de facto* frontiers in Europe and renounced the use of force. The role of NATO in this new context was obscure, not only were the politics of confrontation fading into the background but the common front was once again being split by bilateral treaties and agreements.

Since Article 13 of the NATO treaty gave any member the right to withdraw from the alliance after twenty years, it is probable that there would have been pressure from other countries, besides France, to exercise this right, had it not been for the Soviet invasion of Czechoslovakia in 1968. The ruthless military suppression of free speech and dissent was a sharp reminder to all the NATO allies that talk of political and military realignment in Europe was still very premature. It certainly squashed any moves to try and disband the alliance in the short-term. Nevertheless the political climate has changed and this is reflected in military strategy and planning. NATO is no longer the only forum for developing western Europe's defence strategy. The United States has increasingly tended to bypass its European allies in military talks with the Soviet Union and, in 1975, a European Security Conference was held in Helsinki largely at Russia's instigation, which has been heralded as the greatest single step towards military détente in Europe this century. NATO no longer wields the decisive influence over west European foreign policy that it did for the first twenty years after the end of the Second World War. In defence, as opposed to economic matters, western Europe acts with less rather than more cohesion, and further integration in this area is likely to come as an extension of the supranational economic institutions.

The Contributions of the OEEC and NATO to European Integration

Originally the OEEC and NATO were both very largely manifestations of the United States view of Europe in the late 1940s. They were two powerful organizations mainly financed with American money and, in the case of NATO, sustained with American manpower. Inevitably, therefore, both tended to foster and promote a federal view of Europe. It is a view which the individual European states found attractive economically and necessary militarily, but politically they treated it with considerable reservation.

In the immediate post-war period western Europe was financially bankrupt and politically disorganized and demoralized. For the first few years of their existence the OEEC and NATO instilled a remarkable sense of unity and purpose into a very disparate group of countries, some of which had faced each other in two major wars in the space of thirty years. If they had achieved nothing else, the two organizations would have put forward a strong argument for further co-operation between European states. Throughout the 1950s however they re-emphasized the advantages of political and economic stability. In the post-war era Europe accumulated unprecedented wealth and was able to consolidate its political institutions more successfully than at any time in the previous hundred years. By the end of the decade the question was not whether integration should continue, but what form it should take?

The role of the OEEC and NATO was, nevertheless, essentially introductory. Once European self-confidence began to re-emerge and the individual countries began to find their own voices once more, both organizations became relatively less important. The OEEC was translated into the more international OECD, and NATO became just one of a number of strands in the complex amalgam of European foreign policies.

4

Comecon: The Leitmotif for Integration in Eastern Europe

The Context

The Council for Mutual Economic Assistance, or Comecon as it is more usually referred to in English, was founded on 22 January 1949, with the publication of a joint communiqué by the governments of Bulgaria, Hungary, Poland, Rumania, Czechoslovakia and the USSR. It was a brief statement, only about 400 words in length, but it set out in clear and unequivocal language the aims and objectives of the new organization. The main objective was to further enhance the already close economic relations between the member countries and to increase the general level of trade, as a means of accelerating the reconstruction of their war-torn national economies. Great emphasis was laid on the need for each national economy to be independent. Marshall Aid and the European Recovery Programme were specifically rejected, because they represented undue interference in national sovereignty and would, it was claimed, eventually undermine the economic independence of individual states. The means for achieving the economic expansion and co-operation which Comecon sought to initiate could not rely on any form of supranational government or management, and the communiqué emphasized that the organization's role was to be purely advisory. It was to facilitate the exchange of economic information and technical expertise and to encourage trade in basic raw materials, foodstuffs and machinery on a bilateral, rather than a multilateral basis. The total rejection of centralized control was further underlined by the categorical statement that decisions could only be taken with the full agreement of all interested countries. Although the initial signatories, with the exception of the Soviet Union, were European states, the communiqué made it quite

clear that membership was open to any nation which accepted the
aims of the organization. Exactly how Comecon was to be run was
hardly mentioned at all, except to say that the Council of delegates
from each member country would meet periodically in each national
capital in turn.

Over the years Comecon has gradually developed into a fully
fledged international organization. Albania became a member later in
1949 and East Germany followed in 1950, so that all the east European Communist states were included, with the exception of Yugoslavia. After much protracted negotiation with the Asian Communist
states Mongolia became a full member in 1962 and ten years later, in
1972, Cuba was admitted, giving the organization a foothold in Latin
America. Throughout the whole period the only state to withdraw was
Albania in 1962.

Yet despite the steady increase in membership, Comecon remains
essentially a European organization, bound by the terms of its founding communiqué. It is still almost devoid of supranational authority
and must act, by and large, in an advisory capacity. One of the main
reasons for setting up the organization in the first place was simply to
provide the Soviet Union with a propaganda counter to the European
Recovery Programme; it was never intended originally that the
organization should have real substance. The political reality of the
situation facing the east European countries in 1949 made a mockery
of the fine phrases about preserving the integrity of national sovereignty, for at that time they were all almost completely dominated by
the Soviet Union. Since the early 1960s, however, individual states
have come to enjoy a measure of independence, particularly in the
management of their economic affairs, but in exercising these rights
they have also tended to inhibit the development of Comecon itself
as a separate instrument of economic management.

The response to the challenge of Marshall Aid is not the only
instance of events in western Europe influencing the way in which the
organization developed. The setting up of the European Economic
Community and Euratom coincided with a sudden revival of interest
in Comecon as an international economic organization. Once again
it is certain that the developments in the west sparked off a reaction in
the east, although the link was nowhere near as strong as in 1949.
Nevertheless it is neither fair nor accurate to depict the evolution of
Comecon solely, or even primarily, as a series of hurried counters to
major political and economic initiatives in western Europe. Although
frequently tied down by its initial terms of reference, Comecon has
still managed to act as the springboard for a whole series of other

organizations concerned with political and economic integration, both in eastern Europe and in the Communist world in general.

Emphasizing the importance of national sovereignty was not just a short-term political gambit, dictated by the interests of the Soviet Union in 1949, there were also strong historical arguments in its favour. During the first half of the twentieth century the political history of most of eastern Europe had been markedly different to that of the west. Before the First World War the area was divided among four much larger entities – Tsarist Russia, the Austro-Hungarian Empire, the Prussian Empire and the Ottoman Empire – all of which disappeared after 1919, to be replaced in eastern Europe by a succession of small independent kingdoms and republics. The new political units were completely out of touch with the earlier economic realities. Governments found themselves suddenly responsible for industries with capacity far in excess of their individual domestic markets and, at the same time, cut off from their former hinterlands. There was an urgent need for drastic rationalization and reorganization. Given the general economic climate of the inter-war period this task almost inevitably fell to governments rather than the private sector. The Depression produced widespread bank failures in all the newly formed states, so that government was the only agency with either the money or the power to protect the vestiges of the economy. High tariff walls were quickly erected to protect domestic industries and government money was poured into ailing firms. Thus, even though none of the east European states was at this stage governed by the Communists, there was already a large measure of state control over the means of production.

The events of the Second World War further undermined the role of the private sector. All the countries of eastern Europe were part of the Nazi war machine, either as allies of Germany or as part of the occupied territory of the Third Reich. Although the German war economy was never so highly centralized as that of the United Kingdom, private enterprise was virtually eliminated in all the dependent territories.[1] Wherever possible assets were expropriated and German administration imposed compulsorily at every level. After 1945 the effects of the Jewish emigration and massacre, together with the expulsion of Germans from eastern Europe, made further serious inroads into the viability of the private sector by removing large sections of the educated, managerial personnel. More extensive government control was virtually the only option open, if industry was to survive at all.

Given these circumstances, it is hardly surprising that nearly all the post-war governments in eastern Europe passed legislation for wide-spread agrarian reform and total nationalization of industry. The process was accelerated by the succession of Communist-led coups, but the takeover would certainly have occurred even without this added impetus. By 1950 state ownership was complete almost every-where, the exception being peasant agriculture. Obviously there was little enthusiasm for undoing the effects of such a major economic upheaval, when Comecon was created in 1949, and this was probably just as important as opposition to the Marshall Plan in explaining the insistence in the initial communiqué on preserving the national sovereignty of all the member states.

Paper existence 1949–55

For the first six years of its existence Comecon was little more than a name. There were few formal meetings of the Council and minimal tangible evidence of co-operation, let alone attempts at integration. The overriding cause of the general lack of activity was the single-minded determination of the Soviet Union to create microcosms of its own centrally planned economy in each of the Communist east European countries; multilateral co-operation played no part in its design.

National autarchy and economic self-sufficiency were the basis of the Soviet system, but, despite the widespread state intervention described above, it was not the economic future that many east European states envisaged for themselves after 1945. Czechoslovakia and Poland, the two most industrially advanced countries, had strong traditional links with the market economies of western Europe and initially were set to accept Marshall Aid, until faced with a Soviet veto. Yugoslavia also wished to develop its economy according to the market pattern and insistence on this eventually led to the rift with the Soviet Union and expulsion from the Cominform in 1948.[2] Else-where opposition was less organized and vocal, but introducing the new regime still required a considerable effort on the part of the Soviet Union. It was therefore simplest for them to export their economic structure in its entirety to the newly incorporated satellites, rather than trying to modify it to accommodate different national aspirations.

The key to the Soviet system of economic planning was the medium-term plan, and all the east European states quickly pro-duced plans according to the Soviet model. Bulgaria and Czecho-slovakia were the first in the field in 1949, followed by Hungary and

Poland in 1950 and Albania, East Germany and Rumania in 1951. Each of the plans was for a five-year period, except for the Polish one, which ran for six years. The newly formed Comecon was not involved in either the formulation or the co-ordination of these plans.[3] The unshakable pursuit of autarchy meant that they were for all practical purposes identical and therefore complementary, leaving little or no scope for international co-ordination. Each reflected the Soviet belief that the only secure basis for economic growth was a strong heavy industrial base, and the emphasis was everywhere on metallurgy and heavy engineering, together with the mining and energy industries to create the necessary raw materials. Not surprisingly such development fitted neatly into Soviet medium-term planning. Stalin was obsessed by the need to amass the largest possible stocks of heavy industrial goods for the purposes of defence and if he could draw on supplies from seven additional economies so much the better. The massive reparations demanded from all the east European countries meant that he already had a direct call on a large part of their production. In any case the duplication and overproduction were such that the USSR was the only market for most of the goods.

The east European countries themselves were well aware of the dangers of duplication through lack of co-ordination, and between 1946 and 1948 they set up a number of joint planning committees, well before Comecon had even been thought of as a separate entity. Links were established between Czechoslovakia and Poland, Albania and Yugoslavia, Czechoslovakia and Hungary, Bulgaria and Yugoslavia, Bulgaria and Rumania, and Hungary and Yugoslavia. In 1948, however, the Soviet Union squashed and effectively banned such consultation for running counter to its autarchic principles. If Stalin had had his way the excuse of reparations would have been used to dismantle the bulk of east European heavy industrial structure and to absorb it directly into a single Soviet economy, but such excesses were avoided in the event. Instead most heavy industrial plant was left *in situ*, but managed as a part of Soviet-owned corporations, producing goods for domestic consumption in the USSR. There were two further reasons why economic reconstruction was so heavily biased towards heavy industry. In 1948 NATO countries were banned from exporting virtually all engineering products to eastern Europe or the Soviet Union for reasons of strategic security. The action confirmed Stalin's belief that self-sufficiency in this area was essential and, when the Korean War broke out in 1950, gave him a double excuse for concentrating even more intensively on the heavy industrial sector of the economy.

The major difference between the Soviet-style planned economy
and the market economy, which exists generally in the western
industrial world, is the absence of money as the main medium of
international exchange. General convertibility between the rouble
and the various other currencies of eastern Europe did not exist after
the war and, in contrast to western Europe, attempts to liberalize
money movements were actively resisted. In place of the money
market a system of material balances was used, whereby the output
of raw materials was matched with manufacturing capacity, which in
turn was matched with demand, but all without the regulating
mechanism of money as a common indicator. The operation of the
system is obviously extremely complex, but Kaser has given a clear
account of how it works:

> In the Soviet practice of material balancing, the output of an industry –
> say, coal, – is allocated to other users; these other users calculate the
> output of their product which is feasible with that coal (and other in-
> puts similarly passed to them – in the case of steel, say, iron ore and
> limestone). By applying 'transformation coefficients' (the tons of coal,
> ore and limestone needed per ton of steel), a planned output is calculated
> and this output in turn, is allocated to other users. The users would
> include the coal industry, which then applies its own transformation
> coefficients to verify that it could produce the draft plan of coal. If an
> imbalance is shown (e.g. not enough steel to support the mine-sinking
> programme to exact the planned coal output), the procedure must be
> repeated ('iterated') with variant figures[4].

On the face of it, planning at both a national and an international
level would seem to be an essential ingredient for operating a system
of material balances. National plans ought to be the key to domestic
production and consumption, and central co-ordination of their aims
and objectives the basis for determining foreign trade flows. Unfortunately the theory rarely worked out in practice, the reality all too
often being over-production in one sector, shortages in another and
the general stagnation of foreign trade. The basic difficulty was how
to calculate the material balance equations in practice. Clearly they
cannot be used in a disaggregated form for planning, because each is
compiled in different units, yet if translated into money equivalents
they still produce a distorted picture. Even with the most careful
analysis, material balances can only account for part of the total cash
flow in a firm; numerous items in the production process are omitted.
In other words, it proved virtually impossible to build physical models
of material flows at plant level, let alone the national or international
levels. In addition to this fundamental impasse, there was the fact that
the planning horizon for all the east European economies in the early

1950s was five, or even six years. Long-term planning at the national scale is extremely hazardous under any conditions, but with a system of material balances it proved impossible. The net effect on the planning process was to ensure that short-term objectives invariably took precedence over longer-term ones, because there was some chance of their being realized.

The scope for an organization like Comecon in such a situation was strictly limited. Given the close similarities between the various economies and the problems they faced in organizing their domestic production, there was little point in pursuing the goal of international co-operation and integration. In any case foreign trade, except with the Soviet Union, was at a low ebb and the system of central planning did little to encourage it. In the market economies of the west the bulk of foreign trade arose from manufacturers actively seeking sales, rather than trying to dispose of surplus output, as happened initially in the centrally planned economies. The somewhat unpalatable truth was that planning on the basis of material balances produced goods for which there was frequently no demand and as a result was a poor mechanism for stimulating trade and economic co-operation.

Rigid adherence to autarchic centralized economic planning, with priority to heavy industry was required of all the east European states by the Soviet Union until Stalin's death in 1953. Subsequently, however, there was a slow, but significant relaxation and greater scope was given to individual governments to pursue their own interpretation of national self-sufficiency. A number of factors, besides the removal of Stalin, contributed to the change of policy. With the end of the Korean War there was a general lessening of political tension in the world: the NATO embargo on trade with the Communist bloc was lifted, except for a few items, thus reopening the possibility of selling to western markets; the arguments for the overwhelming concentration on heavy industry were also very much weaker, in view of the reduced defence requirements. In response to the changed circumstances, the Soviet government began to withdraw the more blatant sanctions it had traditionally exercised over the east European economies. War reparations, a serious drain on the resources of all the countries, were formally ended and the Soviet-owned corporations, set up in the late 1940s, were wound up and the assets handed back to the individual national governments.

The impact in eastern Europe was a gradual shift in industrial resources from heavy industry towards consumer goods industries and the reopening of bilateral negotiations on trade. Naturally, in view of the considerable variation in the levels of economic development not all the countries reacted to the changed circumstances in the same way. In general it was the more highly industrialized states – Poland, Hungary, Czechoslovakia and East Germany – that embraced the new opportunities most eagerly, while Rumania, Bulgaria and Albania, which were still predominantly agrarian peasant societies, held back. Nevertheless all the east European countries, even those with reservations, entered into new bilateral trade agreements after 1954.

Throughout all the activity Comecon remained a shadowy presence. Although the Council met twice in 1954, after a break of over three years, the influence it exerted on the new developments is far from clear. Certainly it adhered very strictly to its advisory and consultative role, but it seems probable that it was the forum through which the new bilateral agreements were concluded, in which case its contribution was far from insignificant. There was also another side to its operations. The organization did have a small permanent secretariat in Moscow and this office continued to work at implementing the early decisions of the Council, despite the lack of further formal sessions. For reasons explained above, there was little trade between the European members of Comecon in the organization's early years, but what there was required some form of bilateral balancing and Comecon performed this function. The organization also secured agreement among the members on uniform standards of quality, delivery, packing, payment and guarantees for all exports and imports within the group. Nevertheless, at best these activities only kept the organization ticking over during the first six years. It was out of tune with the main thrust of economic events, most of which were directed towards autarchy and national self-sufficiency, and defining economic relationships with the Soviet Union. It is hard to see the initial establishment of Comecon as anything other than a Soviet propaganda exercise, in reply to the grand design of the European Recovery Programme and the OEEC in the west.

Experiments in Multilateralism

After 1955 Comecon began to be taken far more seriously. A whole series of decisions were made, which infused some life and substance into the organization and, by the end of the decade, it looked as though it would play a central role in the future economic management of both eastern Europe and the Soviet Union. The full story of why it was decided to revive Comecon, rather than create a completely new organization, at that particular time, is not entirely clear.

Probably the fact that Comecon existed in such a rudimentary form ensured that, on the one hand, past precedent would not inhibit future decisions, while on the other, it could be claimed that the organization represented continuity in integrated planning at an international level. The latter point was important, for as with the initial declaration in 1949, the tide of events in western Europe undoubtedly had a strong influence on the timing of the revival, if not the revival itself. The Soviet Union and all the European Comecon members were alarmed at the potential loss of markets, which might have resulted from the imposition of a common external tariff by the newly formed European Economic Community, and the proposal to establish Euratom seemed to postpone the Soviet ideal of a nuclear-free zone in Europe even further into the future. Once more a gesture was required and Comecon, which had already been partially resuscitated, was again the ideal vehicle. The main difficulty was the self-evident disparity between theory and practice. Although all the members of Comecon were supposedly equals, the dictatorial dominance of the Soviet Union was obvious to all. After the brutal way in which the popular risings in both Poland and Hungary had been summarily repressed by the USSR, a tangible concession towards equality was essential. Accordingly, in the late autumn of 1956 the Soviet government put out a declaration in which some of the more flagrant injustices against the east European states were rectified. All the outstanding property claims in areas incorporated into the USSR during the Second World War were to be settled forthwith; the rights of east Europeans stranded in those territories by the occupation were to be restored, including the right of repatriation; consular services were to be improved; the scope and powers of the individual national judiciaries were to be precisely defined; and finally Soviet garrisons were to be reduced everywhere (except in Hungary) and the remaining troops to be stationed under clearly defined terms and guarantees. These political gestures enabled the enhanced Comecon to measure up on more equal terms to the European Economic Community and Euratom. It would however be a gross oversimplification to draw too close a parallel between 1949 and 1956. While rejection of Marshall Aid was almost certainly the most important reason for establishing Comecon, the need to respond to the Rome Treaties was only an extra incentive to a more general move to create a multilateral rather than a bilateral approach to economic management in eastern Europe in the mid-1950s.

The chief concern of all the east European Communist states after 1955 was industrial specialization, or, as they referred to it, the international division of labour, and it was to Comecon they turned for a solution. One of the hallmarks of the Stalinist period had been the steadfast refusal to allow any specialization at the national level, but with the gradual reduction of emphasis on heavy industry and the expansion of consumer goods industries, the inherent wastefulness of duplication became clearer. There was mounting pressure, especially from the more industrialized countries, for some form of international agreement on specialization. Comecon was the obvious forum for discussing the whole question and, after 1955, the subject was clearly on the agenda at the periodic Council meetings.

In the first instance progress was rather slow, not least because Comecon was still restricted to its purely advisory role. Positive action required separate bilateral or multilateral agreements between the states concerned. However, after 1957, the tempo and the general sense of urgency surrounding the discussions increased considerably and by 1961 there was not a single major branch of industry that had not had its prospects for specialization thoroughly debated. The greatest progress was made in the fields of engineering, metallurgy and chemicals. In all three cases the allocation procedure was developed from a complex array of bilateral agreements into a genuinely multilateral system of planning with co-ordination between all the countries involved. For example, agreements such as the one between East Germany and Poland on the manufacture of electrical equipment in 1957 eventually led to more complex allocations, such as the agreement on rolling mill equipment, quoted by Kaser. The agreement was reached at the twelfth session of the Council at Sophia in 1959 and it divided production in the following way: Czechoslovakia and the USSR were allocated the large-scale rolling mills, East Germany and Poland the small-scale ones, and wire-drawing plant was to be located in East Germany and Hungary.[5] Many other similar examples could be quoted, and there is no question that the whole programme was a considerable success. Nevertheless by no means were all the members equally enthusiastic about the new trend. Bulgaria, Rumania and Albania, because of their relatively low levels of industrialization, tended to be overlooked in the overall allocations. Rumblings of discontent, particularly from Rumania, were a persistent background noise to the negotiations and as time went on both their volume and insistence was to grow.

Despite its more prominent role in general economic planning, Comecon remained essentially a forum for discussion and a source of technical advice and expertise. To this end one of the most important initiatives by the new-style organization was the creation of permanent

Standing Commissions, to study the problems of specific industries and selected economic problems. For example, it set up commissions on chemicals, ferrous metals, coal, agriculture and many other industries, and there were also commissions on economic questions, statistics and foreign trade. The precise function and role of these commissions in the overall structure of Comecon will be discussed later, but it is appropriate at this stage to mention the work of the Commission on standardization.

Agreed common technical standards are a prerequisite for specialization in industrial production, yet no formal moves were made to open discussions on the subject until the Commission was set up in 1962. The matter had been discussed on an *ad hoc* basis whenever individual agreements were being drawn up, but this was a poor substitute for universal standards. It also severely restricted access to export markets in the western world, since products from Comecon countries very often did not match the required technical standards. Since 1962 much progress has been made as a result of the work of the Commission and a special office on standardization has been opened at the Comecon headquarters in Moscow; uniform standards, generally acceptable in world markets, are now the rule.

Despite the considerable progress towards standardization and a higher degree of specialization most of the agreements were still bilateral ones, and there was a widespread feeling that the fundamental principles of resource allocation for maximum efficiency and economic growth ought to be explicitly stated. Work on a document, 'Basic Principles of International Socialist Division of Labour', began at the ninth meeting of the Council at Bucharest in 1958, but agreement proved extremely elusive. The fundamental conflict between the developed and the less developed countries, or, more specifically, between Poland, Czechoslovakia and Hungary on the one hand and Rumania on the other, jeopardized any real progress and repeatedly watered down the proposals. When the document was finally published in 1962 (it was the first major policy statement ever to be published by Comecon as such), it was full of compromise and contradiction, offering no real guidance on the fundamental question of specialization. Essentially it fell between two stools, trying to achieve the impossible feat of improving industrial efficiency within the group as a whole, while at the same time preserving the cherished ideal of national autarchy. It is a conflict which has still to be resolved. Agreements on industrial specialization continue to be negotiated in isolation, and the promise of the late 1950s has failed to materialize. An Hungarian economist, writing about trade in Comecon, wryly concluded in 1972 that 'specialization by products and sectors is yet on a low level in CMEA, in almost all fields of economic activity.'[6]

Without question the development of Comecon as an organization was inhibited by the absence of any formal charter of incorporation and proper terms of reference. Until 1960 the founding communiqué was the organization's sole working document and, once its activities began to expand after 1955, the lack of administrative structure became painfully apparent. As a result, in 1960, a charter was published codifying and formalizing the operational practices that had grown up over the years and establishing an adequate administrative structure.

The charter did not alter the fundamental aims and objectives of Comecon. The basic conflict between increasing economic efficiency through specialization and the need to preserve national sovereignty remained unchanged. However, it considerably expanded the institutional framework, a subject hardly mentioned in 1949. The Council remained as the highest authority and it was to meet at least once a year, rather than 'periodically' as before. Like the Council of Ministers in the European Community, it is a flexible organization. The delegates are chosen by each individual country and their seniority can vary according to the business under discussion. Some Council sessions are effectively meetings of the heads of state of the Comecon countries, while others are at a much more mundane level. Nevertheless the Council is still a purely advisory body and has no powers to implement its decisions on the economic problems facing the member countries.

The Executive Committee founded in 1960 was a completely new departure. It consists of one representative from each country and it must meet at least every other month. Essentially it has a watching brief, ensuring that decisions made in the Council are carried out, and ascertaining that there is no loss of momentum in the work on co-ordinating national plans and improving industrial efficiency. Its role is obviously extremely important, since potentially it gives a degree of continuity to Comecon's operations which had been sadly absent in the past.

The new charter also gave official recognition to the Standing Commissions (see above, page 67). These bodies have been among Comecon's most successful innovations, for not only have they performed a valuable function in their own right, they have also greatly enhanced the international character of the whole organization. The advisory role of the Standing Commissions allows them to fit easily into Comecon's overall terms of reference and, since they were first created in 1956, their number has steadily increased. There are now more than twenty, each staffed by highly qualified technical officials, giving advice both on individual sectors of the economy and on general economic problems. An interesting additional feature of the Standing Commissions is the way they are spread throughout the member countries. Each capital houses the headquarters of at least one, covering areas of special interest to that particular country. Thus the Agricultural Commission has its headquarters in Bulgaria, the Chemical Commission in East Germany and the Coal Commission in Poland, in each case a particular economic strength of the country concerned. As with all the other organs of Comecon, the role of the Standing Commissions is purely advisory, but they have provided a crucial co-ordinating service, eliminating wasteful duplication and unnecessary variation in production methods in all sectors of the economy.

Finally the charter took an important initiative in setting up a proper Secretariat under a chief secretary, to provide the administrative support essential to the work of an international organization such as Comecon. The seat of the Secretariat is in Moscow, where a small central office had been located from the organization's earliest days. The precise size of the administration is not known, but clearly it now provides the co-ordination which ultimately binds the organization together.

The revival and institutional strengthening of Comecon after 1955 was also accompanied by a very considerable increase in its areal scope. The first steps were rather tentative, in that the newcomers were not invited to become full members, but were offered instead observer status. The first country to benefit from the new initiative was Yugoslavia, the only Communist country in eastern Europe that successfully managed to defy Stalin and the Soviet Union in the early 1950s and the only east European state not already a full member. The first session of the Council attended by Yugoslavia was the seventh in Berlin in 1956. As an observer a country could send delegates to all Council meetings, but they were not allowed to take part in debates. With the permission of the Council, however, observers were permitted to participate fully in the work of the Standing Commissions relevant to their interests.

The experiment was a success and similar invitations were quickly issued to other Communist countries outside Europe. China became an observer in 1956, followed by North Korea in 1957 and Mongolia and North Vietnam in 1958. It seemed as though the whole focus of the organization was about to shift away from Europe, towards a huge co-ordinated Communist bloc, spanning the whole of Eurasia. As will be explained (see below, page 76) such hopes were short-lived. None of the non-European observers, except for Mongolia which became a full member in 1962, ever made any important contribution to Comecon's work and the whole initiative fell foul of the bitter Sino-Soviet dispute which came into the open after 1960. Since then membership has been static except for the inclusion of Cuba, first as an observer in 1963 and, since 1972, as a full member. It is a rather unimpressive outcome of a bold attempt to unite the whole of the Communist world under the Comecon umbrella.

The most tangible successes from the period of renewed activity after 1955, at least in the short- and medium-terms, were the joint development projects promoted by Comecon. To start with most of these projects were the result of bilateral negotiations between two members and were simply noted with approval by the Council from the sidelines. One of the first was an agreement between East Germany and Poland in 1957, under which the Germans were to invest in new coal mines in the Bogatynia frontier region of western Poland. It was a tentative beginning, since the area had been part of Germany under the Third Reich and the validity of the Oder–Neisse line as the German–Polish frontier had not been finally decided at that time. East Germany therefore felt that it had some territorial stake in the project, but its success in practice led to a spate of other agreements, along similar lines, involving all the European members but not the USSR.

An important variant and extension of the bilateral development project was the Haldex corporation, set up in 1959 jointly by Poland and Hungary to process the slack on coal waste tips. In this case, rather than one country investing in a development project in another, a joint company has been established and the assets are held and managed in common. The technology for the Haldex process was developed in Hungary and used on the waste tips of the brown coal mines at Tata, northwest of Budapest. However as much better results were possible on richer tips, the Hungarian and Polish governments formed a joint company to apply the new technology to the more valuable waste from the Silesia mines.

The reluctance of the USSR to join in the move towards joint planning projects was due to a reluctance on the part of the Soviet government to commit itself to the sector planning which implicitly lay behind the new trend. Poland, Czechoslovakia and East Germany were all very keen that specialization should be extended, so that one country could concentrate its development into a small number of industries, but the Soviet Union was reluctant to relinquish completely direct control over any individual sector of industry. Nevertheless the Russians could not fail to be impressed by the success of schemes like Haldex, where one nation developed a technology and then exported it to other members. It was not until 1962 that attitudes officially began to change, when Khrushchev publicly declared that under certain circumstances the Soviet Union would be prepared to see some manufactures produced exclusively in other Comecon countries. It was a development that was to have profound repercussions on future co-operation and planning in the group. The incipient rift between Poland and the other developed economies and Rumania was torn wide open, and this time marked the end of the most innovative and active period in Comecon's history.

Parallel to these bilateral investment projects, there was also another form of multilateral planning, but one which did not involve transfers of either money or goods. Three separate transmission schemes were planned under the auspices of Comecon for electricity, oil and gas respectively, and the Soviet Union had no qualms about playing a full part in these from the start. Each scheme was planned jointly, but the national governments were responsible for financing and carrying out all the work on the sections within their territory. Kaser has suggested that Soviet enthusiasm for these projects, as opposed to the strictly industrial ones, may have been influenced by the fact that as the major exporter of oil in the group it was able to tie in the east European economies more closely to its own.[7] However, evidence that this was the reason is scant.

The first of these projects to be started was the Mir Electricity Grid, which was discussed in the Council as early as 1954. Certainly the very inadequate generating potential everywhere in eastern Europe, with the exception of the former territories of the Third Reich in East Germany, Czechoslovakia and Poland, was a serious hindrance to industrial development.[8] There were therefore strong arguments in favour of treating the construction of an international grid as a matter of priority. Nevertheless the discussions were prolonged and it was not until 1959 that the plan was finally approved. Once the go-ahead was given progress was rapid. The main section linking East Germany, Poland, Czechoslovakia and Hungary was completed by 1962 and subsidiary links joining Rumania with Czechoslovakia, Hungary with the Soviet Union and Poland with the Soviet Union were completed soon afterwards. The main control centre was located in Prague. The final section joining Rumania to Bulgaria was delayed for a time, because of the difficulty in crossing the Danube, but this too was completed in 1967. The new network is unquestionably a major achievement and a triumph for Comecon planning, providing every member country with access to an indispensable industrial resource.

The Friendship Oil Pipeline Project to export oil from the Soviet oilfields in the Urals to East Germany and Poland was agreed in 1958. New refineries were built at Plonsk just north of Warsaw and at Schwedt on the river Oder and both were refining Russian crude oil, delivered by the pipeline, at the end of 1964. A branch pipeline was also constructed to take oil to another new refinery near Bratislava which would supply Czechoslovakia and Hungary. Once these pipelines were complete oil supplies to eastern Europe were relatively secure. The northern states were supplied from Russia, while Bulgaria and Hungary as well as Yugoslavia were able to rely on crude oil from Rumania. Once again consultation within the framework of Comecon had produced a piece of coherent international development to the benefit of all the members, and subsequently other similar projects were to follow, notably the Six Nation Gas Project. This project, which was finally concluded in November 1975, involves the export of natural gas from Iran to West Germany, Austria and France, via the Soviet Union and Czechoslovakia.[9] The two Comecon countries are building the sections of the pipeline which cross their respective territories in return for specified amounts of free gas.

Not all the multilateral development projects have proceeded quite so smoothly as those described above. The Rumanian fear of being overshadowed by its industrially more powerful northern neighbours was as manifest in this aspect of Comecon's work as it was in every other. Matters came to a head in the discussions about a scheme to build a dam on the Danube at the Iron Gates gorge between Rumania and Yugoslavia in order to produce hydro-electricity and regulate the flow of the river. The scheme was of direct benefit to Hungary and Yugoslavia, which would be spared serious annual flooding, to Rumania and Bulgaria, which would have water for irrigation and, in addition all four would have access to considerably enhanced electricity supplies. Negotiations began in 1957, but were repeatedly bogged down, first because of the ambivalent attitude of the Soviet Union towards Yugoslav participation and subsequently as a result of Rumanian displeasure with its fellow members in Comecon over other aspects of industrial planning. The upshot is that the scheme is now going ahead under joint Rumanian and Yugoslav guidance, completely outside the context of Comecon, and Rumania has made it quite plain that the snub is intentional.[10] When completed a large part of its electricity will be fed directly into the Mir grid, augmenting the total supplies of the group.

In the last analysis the success of Comecon and its many initiatives in the late 1950s and early 1960s were only partly governed by political arguments between the members. Just as important were the limitations built into the organization itself. One of these, the organization's purely advisory role, has already been alluded to several times, and examples have been cited, showing how any action was dependent on subsequent agreement between the states concerned. There was however another fundamental weakness: the lack of a generally convertible currency and multilateral clearing facilities. These innovations were at the very heart of OEEC's success in western Europe and were the foundation upon which the European Community was later based. Comecon failed to devise an east European equivalent to the European Payments Union and its effectiveness as an international organization has been persistently undermined as a result. An attempt was made in 1957 to introduce multilateral clearing of trade balances, but it made little headway, largely because of failure to agree on a mechanism for carrying over from one year to the next credits and deficits.

The members were well aware of Comecon's shortcomings and all the European countries, with the exception of Rumania, were keen to try to circumvent the limitations imposed by the organization's terms of reference. The most successful solution has been the establishment of a number of organizations, technically separate from Comecon, though in reality closely related both to the organization and its activities. Foremost among these new developments have been what Hewett calls Super Standing Commissions.[11] Based on the Standing Commissions inside Comecon, these new organizations have all the same functions and, in addition the power to make substantial decisions, binding on member governments. The first of these new bodies was Intermetall founded in 1964. Its aim is not only to bring about closer co-operation between the ferrous metal industries in eastern Europe but also to improve conditions for trade in metal goods so that productive capacity can be used as fully and as efficiently as possible. Hewett is enthusiastic about both the achievements and the future prospects of Intermetall in the field of supranational planning,[12] but Ausch, an Hungarian economist, is very much more cautious, arguing that as yet there is too little evidence to be able to evaluate the new body, one way or the other.[13] Whoever is right, there has been sufficient success to persuade the participants to establish more Super Standing Commissions. In addition to

Intermetall, there is now Interkhim for the chemical industries, Interatominstrument for the instrument technology of the nuclear energy industry, the Organization for the Co-operation in the Bearing Industry, and finally an unnamed Commission to promote co-operation in the non-ferrous metal industries.

The members have also made attempts to deal with the problem of creating multilateral clearing facilities outside the immediate framework of Comecon. The International Bank for Economic Co-operation was set up in 1964, and most foreign trade transactions with other member countries are now cleared through it. The only rule is that each country must show a zero balance with all the others as a group at the end of each year. Short-term loans can be negotiated with relative ease to cover a deficit, but the new bank still offers little possibility of raising medium or long-term credit, and it is these latter facilities that are essential if trade is to be given a real stimulus. To all intents and purposes multilateral clearing as it has operated in western Europe since the mid-1950s does not yet exist in the east. It was hoped that the opening of the separate International Investment Bank, the prime aim of which is to finance medium- and long-term investment projects would improve this situation, but so far it has not shown much sign of having the desired effect. The Comecon economy still does not enjoy the flexibility bestowed by free currency convertibility and in consequence trade within the group continues to be extremely sluggish.

The Warsaw Treaty Organization

Strictly speaking the Warsaw Treaty Organization, or, as it is sometimes referred to, the Warsaw Pact, is completely independent of Comecon, but given the enormous significance of defence industries for the economy as a whole it has inevitably exerted an important influence on the latter organization. The Warsaw Treaty was signed in 1955 by all the European members of Comecon, together with the Soviet Union, and was intended as a direct reply to the decision in western Europe that allowed West Germany to join NATO. In practice, as with Comecon in its early years, it made very little immediate difference to the organization of defence in eastern Europe. All the member states of Comecon already had bilateral defence agreements with the Soviet Union and these remained the fundamental basis behind strategic planning.

Slowly however the situation began to change and defence was drawn more into the mainstream of economic planning. In 1957 a formal link was established between the Comecon Standing Commission on Defence and the Economic Committee of the Warsaw Treaty Organization, and joint proposals were formulated for the development of nuclear research, railways and telecommunications. In many ways the prospects for international specialization in the defence industries were brighter than in other sections of the economy, since the benefits of co-operation were more immediate and obvious.

Nevertheless the total impact of the organization on strategic planning remained relatively slight, despite these initiatives. In 1961 the Soviet Union made a determined effort to alter this situation. They proposed reducing the overall strength of Russian forces in eastern Europe and replacing them with joint commands and a much larger infusion of troops from the other Comecon countries. The move was interesting not only for its own sake but also for the reaction it evoked. The east European states were sharply divided on the issue and the split between them was along precisely the same lines as the incipient economic split (see above, page 66). East Germany, at one extreme, was strongly in favour of centralized strategic planning, while Rumania, at the other, was opposed to it on the grounds that it further infringed its national sovereignty.

The precise outcome of the dispute is difficult to determine, owing to the intrinsic secrecy that surrounds strategic planning, but without doubt there has been a marked movement away from the bilateralism of the 1950s. The change in attitude is thrown into sharp relief by comparing the way in which the invasions of Hungary in 1956 and Czechoslovakia in 1968 were organized. Both were exhibitions of naked aggression against relatively minor deviations from the strict letter of the Soviet political, as opposed to economic line, but, in the case of Hungary, Russia alone stepped in to quell the dissidents, whereas in Czechoslovakia it was a joint invasion by Russian, East German, Polish and Hungarian troops, acting in concert as members of the Warsaw Treaty Organization. It would be unwise to read too much into a comparison of just two isolated events, but it is arguable that there has been a definite shift towards multilateralism in strategic planning. Such a conclusion reflects a growing confidence on the part of the Soviet Union in the stability and political maturity of the Communist regimes in east Europe and can only encourage co-operation and joint action in other areas in the future.

The Developing Rifts

Despite the progress made by Comecon in the years after 1955, the organization had to continue its work against several strong undercurrents of tension which always threatened to undermine its achievements. The attempt at extending the scope of Comecon into Asia was an almost total failure. There was rivalry between China and the Soviet Union even before China became an observer in 1956, but it subsequently grew to a state of almost open hostility, which finally flared to the surface in 1962. The underlying cause of the conflict was a fundamental struggle between the two foremost Communist states for leadership of the Communist world, but it manifested itself in a series of separate incidents and the enlarged Comecon was one of the casualties. All the members were forced into a position where they had to choose between one side or the other and the whole process split the organization wide open. In the main the Asian countries sided with China and the European ones with the Soviet Union, but this was not exclusively the case. Not only did North Korea and North Vietnam allow their observer status to lapse along with China, Albania too withdrew from the organization. There is no question that Albania's sympathies were with the Chinese, but the actual circumstances of the withdrawal are far from clear. It would appear that rather than simply resigning the Albanian government failed to make its financial contribution to Comecon in 1962. As a result it received no notification of meetings. In public at any rate, the Albanians feigned surprise and indignation at being left out in this way, but the reaction was probably a token one. The Polish government attempted to mediate, but its efforts were somewhat summarily dismissed and Albania was allowed to depart without further fuss.

In some ways the importance of the Sino–Soviet dispute for the future of Comecon should not be overexaggerated. Albania was the poorest and smallest of the organization's members and was physically isolated from the rest by Yugoslavia. It had gained little from joining and made only a small contribution in return. As far as the Asian observer members were concerned, they had only ever been on the fringes of the organization, so that their presence or absence made little material difference. The reason for the whole issue coming to a head in 1962 was that the Soviet Union was seeking a greater commitment to co-operative planning from all the members and was anxious to remove the somewhat non-committal observer status. Nevertheless the denouement was untidy. There were now two European Communist countries outside the scope of the organization and, in Asia, Mongolia alone sided with the Soviet Union and became a full member in 1962. A less tangible but equally serious result of the dispute was the effect it had on the confidence and commitment of the other members. Comecon had promised a great deal after 1955 but the

results were few and the benefits fragmentary. The doubts and disillusionment of the remaining members, which in some cases had
never been far below the surface, now began to be expressed more
openly.

The internal disagreements essentially revolved around the importance to be attached to national sovereignty, a fundamental issue in
Comecon from its very inception. The effects of the argument have
already been referred to, but from the early 1960s the pressure began
to mount. On the one hand were the developed industrial countries,
led by Czechoslovakia and Hungary; on the other the less developed
agrarian nations, led by Rumania.

The essence of the case made by the industrialized countries was a
demand for relaxation of the system of strict centralist planning and a
move instead towards what has been called the guided market
economy.[14] For practical purposes the one followed from the other,
for the greater co-operation preached by Khrushchev in 1962 would
have been impossible to achieve through the mechanism of material
balances, traditionally used for allocating resources in the centrally
planned economies. As shown above this system was hard pressed to
plan individual national economies efficiently, let alone several
economies jointly.

In the guided market economy, which exists and is working well in
Hungary and was beginning to develop in Czechoslovakia before the
1968 invasion, there is a move away from the complete universality
and rigid centralism which characterize Soviet-style central planning.
The economy as a whole is still programmed by plan, but the document is much less detailed than under the earlier system and usually
consists of a series of general economic objectives rather than precise
instructions to individual plants as before. The most significant
change in the guided market approach to planning, however, is the
virtual abandonment of any attempt at trying to match material
balances. Instead, each enterprise seeks out markets for its products
on its own behalf and sells them at more or less its own price. The
whole system has much in common with the mixed-market economy
of much of western Europe. Its greatest attraction is that it virtually
eliminates the time-consuming and cumbersome process of checking
and cross-checking on material balances, traditionally the main burden
of economic planning in eastern Europe. Even without the direct formal
links between the individual factory and the state, the government is
still able to exert formidable pressure to ensure compliance with its
policies, through strict control of prices and incomes. Indeed, in
reality the means have changed more than the ends, but this did not

stop the guided market economy being viewed with the utmost suspicion by some other members of Comecon.

The chief opponent of any attempt at diminishing the dominant role of the state in economic management was Rumania. Ever since 1955 it had waged a most successful rearguard action against all attempts by other Comecon members, including the USSR, to compromise the principle of national sovereignty and make the role of the organization anything other than advisory. The Rumanian government's objections to supranational planning were straightforward and uncomplicated. It felt the country would never be able to fully industrialize and loosen its heavy dependence on agriculture if it were merged into a single Comecon economy. The relative order would inevitably be maintained, with the Soviet Union and the industrialized countries of eastern Europe at the top of the hierarchy. Rumania's own economic success, particularly in developing trade with western Europe, only served to confirm the belief of the government in the rightness of its policies.

In pursuing these objectives Rumania has successfully frustrated much that the other members have tried to achieve through Comecon. The most important battle was the protracted fight to modify the declaration on industrial specialization, Basic Principles of International Socialist Division of Labour (see above, page 66). From 1958 to 1962 it repeatedly refused to accept any provision which took away from the individual state the right to determine any aspect of industrial policy and, when the document was finally agreed, it was so watered down and full of contradictions as to be of little practical value. Similarly, when the organization agreed its formal charter in 1960, Rumania insisted that the issue of sovereignty should be incorporated as one of the chief principles and purposes of Comecon. However, the real trial of strength came in 1962, when the Soviet Union began to show a more active interest in sectoral planning and the creation of a supranational agency to oversee industrial development. Rumania threatened to leave the organization if the proposal was put into effect and, faced with this situation, the whole idea was dropped. Comecon's role in economic planning remained, and still remains, purely advisory. The other European members of Comecon and the Soviet Union have sought to bypass the impasse by creating the Super Standing Commissions (see above, page 73), outside the formal framework of the organization. Despite their success, Rumania refuses to take part and supranational planning is left in a somewhat fragmented condition.

Although it will have no truck with a supranational planning body,

Rumania has by no means isolated itself from the international scene. It has simply proceeded in its international relations by bilateral rather than multilateral agreement. The most celebrated of the development projects it has negotiated is the Iron Gates Project with Yugoslavia. In a way this too was an act of defiance, since Yugoslavia is not a full member of Comecon, and the move was widely interpreted as a snub to the Soviet Union, which wanted to draw Rumania more closely into the organization. Another fiercely independent act was the assumption of diplomatic relations with West Germany, despite local protests from its Comecon partner, East Germany.

Rumania's fight is important on two counts. First it has been largely successful in frustrating attempts to develop Comecon as an international body, comparable with those in western Europe. Secondly, it has clearly shown the limits to Soviet domination and the extent to which individual states can pursue their own independent line. This is most significant for a proper appreciation of the post-war political climate in eastern Europe.

The invasion of Czechoslovakia in 1968 may appear to invalidate any attempt to generalize from the Rumanian experience, but there is good reason for arguing that it was Czechoslovakia and not Rumania that was the special case. Czechoslovakia in 1968 appeared to be working towards political reforms that would have liberalized its relations with the west to an extent unthinkable in Rumania, which has always remained close to the traditional, pre-war style of Soviet government. Indeed the economic reforms proposed in Czechoslovakia were less radical than measures which had already been enacted and continue to flourish in Hungary. Nonetheless the invasion had a traumatic effect on Comecon. As a direct result the Soviet government abandoned its rather half-hearted flirtation with the guided market economy and returned to its much more rigid, centralized planning procedures, thus further retarding the development of the organization as an international body with real political and economic power.

The Prospects for Integration

The future of integration in the Comecon countries is now at something of a crossroads. The burst of creative energy that exploded after 1955 fizzled out in acrimony, disillusionment and, ultimately after the invasion of Czechoslovakia, bitterness. Yet, if the will is forthcoming, the prospects for closer co-operation are not much less encouraging than in western Europe. The economic disparities in terms of GNP and per capita incomes in Comecon are little different from those in the EEC and EFTA. Portugal is just as poor a relative to the Scandinavian countries as is Bulgaria to Poland and Czechoslovakia, and yet it has enjoyed great benefits from membership of EFTA.

The explanation for the limited success at achieving integration in Comecon must therefore lie elsewhere. Certainly the lack of enthusiasm shown by Rumania in particular has not helped, but this too cannot be the full story. It would seem that the fundamental cause is the practical difficulty of administering a centrally planned economy. The complexities involved in extending the concept into the international area are so great that they have so far effectively defied a solution. The problems have fallen into three major areas. First, the rate of economic growth in all the east European countries has consistently outrun even the most optimistic predictions. In other words, all the techniques for predictive planning have been found wanting at the national, let alone the international level. Secondly, the whole system is far too inflexible. Production targets are matched closely to theoretical capacity, with the inevitable result that they are rarely met, owing to unforseen difficulties. The third problem is the lack of incentive among the planners in each individual country to strive for integration. Unlike the firm operating under the market economy of western Europe which is able to equate larger markets with larger profits, for the planner in eastern Europe larger markets simply mean more work – a powerful disincentive indeed!

There has been a measure of *de facto* integration, especially among the more industrialized countries, as a result of the large number of bilateral agreements and the work of the Super Standing Commissions, but it cannot be compared with the specialization which has occurred generally throughout the western trading nations. Hewett has summed up the situation in the following terms: 'The numerous attempts to encourage plan co-ordination, the Basic Principles, and Khrushchev's proposal for supranational planning were all directed at stimulating increased specialization and trade in CMEA. It appears none has succeeded, and there remains a general agreement that something is wrong in the CMEA economy.'[15] Sharp confirmation of these misgivings was provided by the Czechoslovakian invasion. The reaction of the Soviet Union was to retract all reforms aimed at liberalizing economic management and to insist, more strongly than for several years, on a strict adherence to the principle of centralized planning and government control.

Nevertheless the economic if not the political desirability of greater co-operation was not lost sight of and, in 1969, a series of discussions were initiated within Comecon, to formulate a programme for future action. The results were published in 1971 at the twenty-fifth session of the Council and portentously entitled 'The Comprehensive Programme for the Further Deepening and Improvement of Co-operation and the Development of Socialist Economic Integration of the Member Countries of CMEA.' As its title suggests, it is an ambitious document with a broad field of enquiry. The main topics it considered were the common economic goals of all Comecon countries; the contribution that closer institutional co-operation could make to achieving those goals; the main areas where co-operation might be fruitful; and the legal and organizational difficulties facing any attempt at integration. Unfortunately the detailed proposals were disappointing. As so often with major Comecon policy statements they appeared to be a mass of contradictory statements which could hardly form a solid basis for future action. Admittedly it is as yet too soon to pass a final judgement, but the prospects are not good.

Nevertheless, the achievements of the individual members of Comecon must be seen in perspective. Belittling their attempts at integration because they do not seem to measure up to the economic successes of western Europe in the 1950s and 1960s is an easy but in all probability a rather facile exercise. Admittedly economic growth was slower during this particular period, but it still went ahead at an unprecedented rate. As Kaser says: 'The crucial fact of Comecon's history from its foundation to the present is that the rapid growth of its aggregate production has not been accompanied, as in other world economic groups, by a relatively more extensive international division of labour, either among its members or with the rest of the world.'[16] In the long run, not closing their industrial options through specialization may turn out to be an enormous benefit to the individual Comecon states. With this in mind, it is perhaps worth noting that in 1974 the United Nations statistics on per capita income showed that the East Germans were better off than the British. It is the first time that an east European country has overtaken any of the major industrial economies of western Europe; it remains to be seen whether it will be the last.

5

The Nature and Origins of the European Community

The Motivation

The European Community came into existence as a single entity on 1 July 1967, when the governments of Belgium, France, West Germany, Italy, Luxembourg and the Netherlands, the original signatories of the Treaties of Rome and Paris in the 1950s, agreed to merge the independent executives of the European Coal and Steel Community, the European Economic Community and the European Atomic Energy Community. It was the culmination of twenty years of patient negotiation and co-operation, and the result was a supra-national organization serving the joint interests of a group of previously autonomous states. The event itself was not particularly important, but the decision marked a point of no-return in one of the most significant collaborative ventures in modern European history.

The size and scope of the European Community are impressive, covering an area of 1,708,984 square kilometres and embracing a population of over 270 million. The combined gross national product of the nine member nations is larger than that of either the Soviet Union or the United States, and the organization serves more people. The essence of the experiment is an attempt to fuse broad political and economic objectives and to sink narrow national differences, so as to create a strongly based and competitive platform for participation in world affairs. Even though the Community is still far from being fully developed and in the eyes of much of the world has yet to prove itself, it is, nevertheless, a political and economic force with which to be reckoned.

Success in the venture has been due of course to the interplay of many factors and has come at a time of almost unprecedented change.

82

Indeed the survival of the Community must largely be attributed to the fact that it has filled a political vacuum in Europe. As recently as 1939, before the outbreak of the Second World War, one of the hallmarks of political power and influence was the possession of an extensive overseas empire. Britain, France, Belgium, the Netherlands, Spain, Portugal and Italy all administered colonies which acted as sources of manpower and raw materials for their industries and markets for their manufactures. The existence of these empires allowed the European states a remarkable degree of freedom and independence in their dealings with each other, and often enabled them cavalierly to disregard the advantages of mutual co-operation. The demands of the overseas possessions meant that there was little enthusiasm for time-consuming commitments in Europe itself.

By 1945 the whole situation had been transformed: 'Everywhere the myth of European colonial superiority and the belief in the solidity of European colonial rule were shattered.'[1] Most of the colonial powers had suffered humiliating military defeats in the European war and even the supposed victors were almost totally impoverished as a result of their war efforts. The thirty years since the end of the war have witnessed the final chapter in the colonial saga: virtually all the former colonies have become fully independent nations and now retain little more than sentimental links with the European parent countries. Even preferential trade agreements, such as those organized within the British Commonwealth, are breaking down and being replaced by wider European agreements. For example, the Lomé Convention links forty-six developing countries with the European Community as a whole and most of these associates are former British and French colonial territories.

In many ways the revolution ending colonial rule has been somewhat remote from Europe, but even so it has forced most European states to rethink completely the whole structure of their political and economic relations, both with the world in general and, more especially, with each other. The OEEC and NATO in their different ways illustrated the advantages of closer co-operation, but at the same time the scope and potential of both organizations were severely limited. By safeguarding national sovereignty and making individual governments responsible for implementing virtually all decisions, there was little chance that either organization would achieve true integration and develop common institutions. In any case they were both such large bodies that obtaining the agreement of all parties for detailed policies would have been an impossible task. The force of these limitations became progressively more obvious as time went on.

Those countries wishing to be part of a more truly supranational grouping with independent executive powers became restive and began to look at ways and means of developing separate organizations. It is the results of these new initiatives that have now been merged to form the single European Community.

Early Moves

The cause of European integration has been espoused intermittently for centuries by individuals as different as Erasmus, Kant, Gladstone and Churchill, and there are any number of published exhortations urging closer co-operation between neighbouring states. In general, however, it is a cause which has rarely excited the imagination or the enthusiasm of the population at large. National rivalry has always run too deep, effectively ruling out much real progress towards integration.

During the present century these traditional attitudes have gradually been reversed. The tentative beginnings stretch back to the decision of the Belgian and Luxembourg governments in 1921 to remove all restrictions on trade and commerce between their two countries. Customs unions of this kind have been a common though somewhat transitory feature of the European scene for over a century, so there was nothing particularly unique in this decision. Its importance however lay in the developments which subsequently grew from it. Economically the union was very successful, and other European countries were not slow to take note of its advantages. When the Netherlands started to think about rebuilding its war-ravaged economy, there was a strong incentive for it to join the Belgium–Luxembourg union. The German occupation meant that all three governments were exiled together in London, so that talks about co-operation were unencumbered by the usual day-to-day political pressures, and progress was rapid. The Benelux agreement was signed in 1944, but did not actually come into force until four years later, at the beginning of 1948.

The Benelux agreement is a true customs union, with the emphasis heavily on reducing internal tariffs and presenting a common trade front to the outside world. The simplicity of its aims quickly encouraged other European countries to try and make similar arrangements elsewhere. France and Italy signed a treaty setting up a bilateral customs union called Francita in 1949 and subsequently they tried, abortively, to merge it with Benelux under the all-embracing and somewhat unfortunate title of Fritalux. Elsewhere in Europe negotiations were begun between the Scandinavian countries, Italy and

Austria, and Turkey and Greece, but all eventually petered out. The only one to become an effective economic reality was the Benelux union. Nevertheless the sum of these negotiations, whether or not they were successful, was important for the tone and direction they set. Although the present European Community has much wider political aspirations, its initial efforts have been towards creating a unified economic base and this is due in no small measure to the Benelux union and its still-born siblings.

There were hopes in the late 1940s that the initiative in promoting more broadly based integration in western Europe would be taken by the newly formed Council of Europe. The Council came into existence on 3 August 1949 and its terms of reference, as set out in the founding statute, seemed to provide the ideal platform for furthering the concept of an integrated Europe. The avowed aim was 'to achieve a greater unity between its Members for the purpose of safeguarding and realising the ideals and principles which are their common heritage and facilitating their economic and social progress'.[2] From the outset, however, there were wide differences of interpretation about the manner of achieving this objective. Some countries felt that the Council should strive for true economic and political union; others interpreted the brief more narrowly and merely saw it as committing them to increased inter-governmental co-operation between independent partners. In addition the Council also had many other objectives besides integration. Once it started work uncertainty about the terms of reference and the broad nature of the brief tended to hamper its activities. So far the Council's efforts have been somewhat diffuse, ranging widely through economic, social, cultural, scientific, legal and administrative matters and human rights, without focussing its attention on any one area. Indeed the only subject specifically excluded by the founding statute is all matters relating to national defence, in deference to the neutrality of four of the members. Austria, Eire, Sweden and Switzerland would all have refused to join had there been any suggestion of involvement with military activities. In practice of course the specific exclusion of defence matters is only an extreme example of the more general difficulty of trying to involve a wide membership, while at the same time maintaining scope for useful action. There is always the danger that progress on any issue will be slow and halting, or, as in the case of European integration, non-existent.

The Council of Europe is the most broadly based of all the European organizations. The original signatories were Belgium, Denmark, France, Eire, Italy, Luxembourg, the Netherlands, Norway, Sweden and the United Kingdom, but subsequently they have been joined by Greece (1949), Iceland, Turkey, the Saar and West Germany (1950), Austria (1956), Cyprus (1961), Switzerland (1963) and Malta (1965) (Figure 12). Greece's membership was suspended between 1969 and 1974, when the country was ruled by a military junta, but was then restored with the return of democratic government.

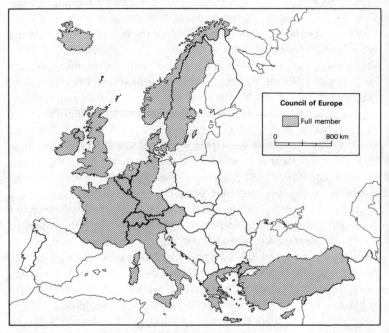

Council of Europe

Full member

0   800 km

Figure 12   Membership of the Council of Europe 1977

The Council operates through a Committee of Ministers and a Consultative Assembly. The Committee of Ministers comprises the Foreign Minister, or his nominee, of each member country and forms the main link with the participating national governments. The Consultative Assembly is made up of 140 representatives, all of whom are nominated by the national governments from among their elected members. Over the years the two bodies have made extensive recommendations on a wide range of issues, notably in the field of human rights, but in essence their role has been consultative. The Council has always had the freedom to act as a kind of west European conscience, as in its defence of human rights, but it has never lived up to the hope of some of the initial signatories that it would take a lead in establishing the institutions necessary for political and economic integration.

The European Coal and Steel Community (ECSC)

The need for a new initiative if further progress were to be made, became increasingly clear as time went on, and it was the French who eventually broke the deadlock in a surprise move, which combined a strong conceptual base with political realism. On 9 May 1950 the Foreign Minister, Robert Schuman, issued a declaration stating that the ultimate aim of French foreign policy over the past twenty years had been a united Europe and that this would continue to be his country's goal, because, in the last analysis, it was the only way in which peace could be maintained. He recognized that it was unrealistic to think of achieving unity in one fell swoop and stated bluntly that an essential prerequisite of any progress was an end to the historical enmity between France and Germany which had led to three major wars in the space of less than a century. He therefore proposed that immediate efforts be directed towards one limited, but crucial objective: the joint management of the entire Franco–German coal and steel production by a High Authority, within a supranational organization open to other European nations.

The 'Schuman Plan', as the proposals came to be known, was bold, imaginative and superbly timed, but although much of its initial success was due to the freshness of its approach, it was in fact the result of many years of careful preparation. The architect of the plan was Jean Monnet, for many years head of the French National Planning Authority. He was the leading protagonist of European political integration and, as early as 1940, had proposed a Franco–British political union. His new idea was to link the concept of international control over heavy industry, which was already being widely canvassed and actually practised in Germany, with the concept of an eventual United States of Europe. Once he had convinced Schuman that the proposal was feasible and in France's best interests, events moved quickly and the plan was adopted as official French government policy.

The alacrity with which the plan was accepted was heavily influenced by the fact that it offered a way out of a difficult political impasse. There was a growing realization that ways would have to be found to reintegrate Germany into the community of European nations and this took on an added urgency with the outbreak of the Korean War. There was a sudden increase in the demand for steel to feed the American war industries, but since it was already in very short supply throughout the western world, there was almost no spare capacity for increased production, either in America or Europe. The sole exception was German heavy industry, which for political reasons was still at a virtual standstill after the war. The Schuman Plan offered a way of bringing this spare capacity back into production, while still maintaining a measure of international control over the uses made of the end product.

The French government issued invitations to several European countries, asking them to take part in a conference to examine the proposals in detail and to produce a draft treaty giving them effect. Five countries – Belgium, West Germany, Italy, Luxembourg and the Netherlands – accepted, but there was one notable absentee. The United Kingdom rejected the proposal from the outset, because it was unwilling to entertain any suggestion of executive control being exercised by an independent, supranational High Authority. The British absence did not inhibit the others however and, on 18 April 1951, they all signed the Treaty of Paris, setting up the European Coal and Steel Community from the end of July 1952.

The fundamental purpose of the Community was to encourage economic expansion, growth of employment and a rising standard of living for the member states, through the establishment of a common market in coal and steel. Specifically, it had to ensure that supplies were adequate and that all parts of the Community had equal access to them; prices were to be kept as low as sound economic management would permit; production potential was to be expanded and improved within the context of a sound policy of resource use; working conditions for employees were to be improved; international trade was to be expanded; and production methods were to be modernized. In general it was a call for the planned, orderly expansion of both industries, but the terms within which the expansion could occur were severely circumscribed. Certain practices were deemed incompatible with a common market and consequently were to be phased out by the High Authority. Chief among these were import and export controls, quantitative restrictions, price discrimination, state subsidies and market sharing. In practice this defined the main executive responsibilities of the ECSC, for later in the treaty it stated quite categorically that once the conditions for free competition had been established there was to be as little market intervention as possible. In retrospect it is clear that the original brief was very much a product of the particular economic conditions affecting the coal and steel industries in the early 1950s. Demand for both products considerably exceeded supply and the Treaty of Paris set out the conditions for maximizing production in a free market economy. The programme was essentially negative and non-interventionist in economic terms and certainly not geared to deal with the problems of overproduction and stagnation, both of which were to plague the coal and steel industries throughout the greater part of the 1960s.

One of the most interesting and important aspects of the ECSC was the nature of its structure and organization. Being the first of the truly supranational European organizations with executive functions, it naturally had a profound influence on the organizations that were to follow it. The chief executive body was the High Authority, located in Luxembourg. It consisted of nine members, appointed by the constituent governments for a period of six years, and a permanent staff. The High Authority was responsible for the day-to-day running of the Community's business. To do this it naturally required considerable funds which were raised by levies on all coal and steel production. The levies were paid direct to the High Authority, but they were not allowed to exceed one per cent of the average value of production without the consent of the Special Council of Ministers. In fact, although the initial level was 0·9 per cent, it was subsequently reduced by a series of stages until it reached 0·2 per cent. Thus the High Authority not only had powers of direct intervention in the coal and steel industries, it could also levy taxes, both powers which had previously been the exclusive preserve of national governments. However its ultimate independence was limited by the lack of effective powers of enforcement. It is true that it could withhold funds from firms which did not comply with the regulations, but the sums were not large enough to have much effect one way or the other. In practice it relied on national governments to compel compliance in those areas where it was necessary. What the ECSC achieved therefore was really supranational control by consent.

Naturally there were also more direct checks and balances on the executive built into the Community. A Consultative Committee of fifty-one members, drawn from producers, workers and consumers, kept the High Authority in touch with the main groups directly affected by its work. The Special Council of Ministers, consisting of one ministerial representative from each member country, had the job of liaising between the High Authority and the national governments. As the ECSC developed the Special Council of Ministers became the ultimate authority to which the executive was responsible and, in this sense, it was the most powerful organ of the Community. The legal interpretation of the Treaty of Paris was undertaken by the Court of Justice, an international court with members drawn from all the constituent countries. The governmental structure of the ECSC was completed by the Common Assembly, which consisted of seventy-eight members nominated by the national governments from among their

democratically elected parliamentarians. They received reports from
the High Authority about its activities, but as the Assembly had no
legislative powers and could only censure the executive after it had
acted, its influence on the working of the Community was strictly
limited. Despite the variation in the control that they were able to
exercise, these four institutions made the ECSC a very broadly based
body, with a capacity for adapting to changing conditions as the
organization developed.

The European Defence Community (EDC)

It would be quite wrong to give the impression that progress towards
European integration has proceeded smoothly in the countries of the
Six without internal opposition and openly expressed doubts. Hardly
had the ECSC come into full operation before proposals were being
considered for a European Defence Community. Superficially it was
similar in structure and concept, but on closer inspection it involved
a much stronger commitment to political union, and on these grounds
was widely criticized and eventually rejected.

Once again the architect of the proposal was Jean Monnet and his
basic aim was the further reintegration of West Germany through the
medium of a combined European army, under European rather than
national leadership. Unlike ECSC however this proposal from the very
beginning was ruled out by events. With the outbreak of the Korean
War in 1950, there were increased fears of a Soviet attack on western
Europe and the feeling was widespread that some mechanism should
be found to enable West Germany to make a military contribution to
NATO. German rearmament was of course still an extremely sensitive
issue and a complete anathema to the French. The EDC seemed on
the face of it to provide an acceptable compromise.

As with the ECSC, the French again took the first formal initiative.
Using Monnet's ideas, the Prime Minister, René Plevan, presented
'the Plevan Plan' for a European Defence Community to the French
National Assembly in October 1950. The United Kingdom was once
more invited to participate, but again firmly refused. The Six therefore went ahead and, notwithstanding considerable internal opposition particularly in France, signed a draft treaty setting up the EDC
in Paris in May 1952.

The structure of the EDC was very similar to that of the ECSC.
The main executive body was the Board of Commissions, with similar
though rather more circumscribed powers than the High Authority of
the ECSC. The Council of Ministers, on the other hand, was a rather

stronger body than the Special Council of Ministers in the ECSC, capable of exercising much more direct control over the workings of the executive. As an interim measure it was agreed that the Common Assembly should act as the parliamentary organ of the EDC as well as of the ECSC, until such a time as proposals were worked out for a more broadly based European Political Community. Discussions went ahead in conjunction with the Consultative Assembly of the Council of Europe and, in 1953, the two bodies produced a joint report recommending the setting up of a single European Community, embracing foreign policy, defence, industry and trade. The speed at which integration was progressing was phenomenal and it seemed that nothing could prevent the emergence of a federal United States of Europe within a matter of a few years.

At this point the whole venture suddenly began to founder. Ratification of the EDC treaty by individual national parliaments was proceeding slowly and amidst heated controversy; the initial ostensible reason for the EDC, the Korean War had ended; and, in the Soviet Union, Stalin had died, thus somewhat defusing the Cold War. By 1954 neither France nor Italy had managed to ratify the treaty and, when a vote was taken in the French National Assembly on 30 August 1954, it was rejected. It was a turn of events which effectively killed both the EDC and the wider European Political Community. Although the end came suddenly, popular public support for both proposals had been waning gradually for some considerable time. The erosion of national autonomy was greater than the majority of the population, particularly in France and Italy, were prepared to countenance. They preferred to wait and see first of all how the ECSC worked out in practice.

The rejection was a serious blow to the cause of European integration, calling into question as it did the whole philosophy behind the movement. There was general agreement that something ought to be salvaged from the wreckage, and in September 1954, it was decided to revive the Brussels Treaty Organization and to develop an independent European defence initiative, with the full participation of the United Kingdom and incorporating both Italy and West Germany. The result was the Western European Union, which came into existence on 6 May 1955 (Figure 13).

The Western European Union began auspiciously, organizing the 1955 referendum which saw the Saar incorporated into West Germany. The early promise was not fulfilled, however, for it was soon clear that its functions conflicted with those of NATO and inevitably the latter emerged as the more senior organization of the two. The

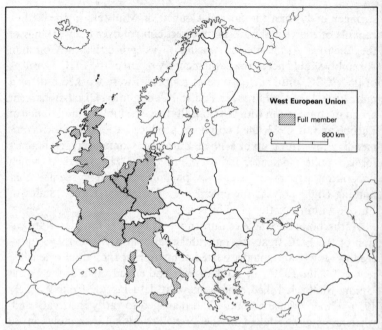

Figure 13   Membership of the West European Union 1977

Western European Union gradually faded into the background, functioning only as a consultative body. In the late 1950s and early 1960s it was revived briefly as a bridge organization between Britain and the Six, but even here its role was relatively unimportant. Now that the European Community itself is more firmly established and includes the United Kingdom, the role of the Western European Union appears to be even more peripheral to the mainstream of political events.

The European Economic Community (EEC)

Not surprisingly the Six required a little time to regroup and recover from the acrimonious shambles of the EDC, but nevertheless within three years they had signed major new treaties establishing the European Economic Community and the European Atomic Energy Community, both with effect from 1 January 1958 (Figure 14).

The successful emergence of the EEC was a tribute to the growing spirit of compromise among the Six. Each country felt that it had something different to gain from the union and was determined to fight as hard as it could for its own interests and aspirations. In simple

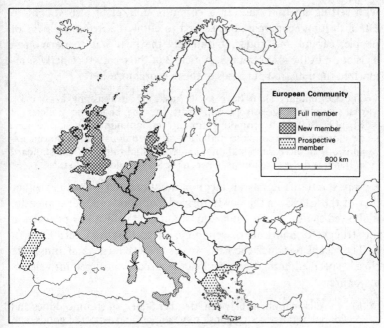

Figure 14   Membership of the European Communities 1977

terms the success of the EEC depended on the French and the Germans agreeing to a compromise, Italy being economically too weak to exert much influence and the other three members too small. The French economy and especially French agriculture had traditionally been protected from foreign competition by an extensive and complicated network of tariffs and quotas. As a result the French viewed free trade within the Community somewhat warily. The Germans, on the other hand, were eager to enlarge the tariff-free market for their industrial goods. The solution which satisfied all parties was a tariff-free market within the countries of the Six and a common external tariff for all imports from third countries. In addition it was agreed that there should be a common agricultural policy to protect all threatened farming interests. This was a major concession to the French, as was the agreement whereby all France's overseas possessions were admitted to special associate status within the Community.

The Treaty of Rome faithfully reflected these different emphases and interests. In preliminary discussions the nascent organization was universally referred to as the Common Market, but in the treaty itself the title European Economic Community was used. The change emphasized the broad scope of the treaty; not only was it concerned with setting up free trade in a common market, it also sought to establish joint economic policies and to allow the free movement of people, capital and goods. Ultimately the goal was to harmonize legislation in the six countries. Article 2 of the treaty succinctly summarized the aims and purposes of the new organization:

> The Community shall have as its task, by establishing a common market and progressively approximating the economic policies of Member States, to promote through the Community an harmonious development of economic activities, a continuous and balanced expansion, an increase in stability, an accelerated raising of the standard of living and closer relations between the States belonging to it.[3]

By any standards it was an incomparably broader brief than either that of the ECSC or the newly formed Euratom and, consequently, it allowed the EEC to assume almost automatically a key position in the struggle for political and economic integration in western Europe.

The means by which the EEC was to achieve its general aims were closely specified in the treaty and can be broadly grouped into eleven major areas:

(a) the elimination, as between Member States, of customs duties and of quantitative restrictions on the import and export of goods, and all other measures having equivalent effect;

(b) the establishment of a common customs tariff and of a common commercial tariff towards third countries;

(c) the abolition, as between Member States, of obstacles to freedom of movement for persons, services and capital;

(d) the adoption of a common policy in the sphere of agriculture;

(e) the adoption of a common policy in the sphere of transport;

(f) the institution of a system ensuring that competition in the common market is not distorted;

(g) the application of procedures by which the economic policies of Member States can be co-ordinated and disequilibria in their balance of payments remedied;

(h) the approximation of the laws of Member States to the extent required for the proper functioning of the common market;

(i) the creation of a European Social Fund in order to improve employment opportunities for workers and to contribute to the raising of their standard of living;

(j) the establishment of a European Investment Bank to facilitate the economic expansion of the Community by opening up fresh resources;

(k) the association of overseas territories and countries in order to increase trade and to promote jointly economic and social development.[4]

The variety and complexity of this list of activities illustrates how ambitious a concept the EEC was in comparison with the other supranational bodies. The Paris Treaty, for example, made much of the fact that the ECSC was to be more than merely a common market in coal and steel, but it did not specify the precise nature of the additional activities. The Treaty of Rome establishing the EEC was quite different. By spelling out not only aims and objectives, but also the manner in which they were to be achieved, the organization was endowed with a unique coherence and sense of direction.

Nevertheless, as in most organizations, running the EEC in practice has been an exercise in the art of the possible. Inevitably it proved difficult for both political and economic reasons to accord from the outset equal weight to all eleven areas of interest. In the first instance the main effort was directed towards establishing the 'Bases of the Community' – the free movement of goods; a joint policy for agriculture; the free movement of persons, services and capital; and a common transport policy. Action in these fields was deemed to be essential if the EEC was ever to be properly established, and they were therefore treated as priority areas. In the event it has proved very difficult to make much real progress even in some of these priority areas, and the development of the EEC has been much hindered in consequence. The operation of the more important individual key policies is the subject of Chapter 8, but it is appropriate at this point to give a more generalized and broader overview of the Community's activities, so as to illustrate the extent to which policies and priorities were modified by events.

The cornerstone of the EEC has been the common market and the common external tariff. Despite its pretensions at being more than just a trading arrangement between member countries, these were the *sine qua non* of the organization. A precise timetable for achieving both objectives was laid down in the treaty itself. Internal restrictions were to be reduced in six stages over a twelve-year period, so that by 1 January 1970 all artificial barriers to trade between the Six would have disappeared. In fact progress was more rapid than even the most optimistic forecasts. By 1 January 1965 tariffs within the Community had been reduced by 70 per cent and by 1 July 1968, eighteen months ahead of schedule, they had been completely abolished. Work on the common external tariff governing imports from third countries also proceeded smoothly and was completed at the same time. A further cause for congratulation was the rate of the external tariff, which was much lower than envisaged in the treaty, owing to the successful negotiations to reduce tariff levels generally among the western trading nations as part of the Kennedy Round.[5] In this sense the EEC got off to a flying start, since its first major objective was being pursued at a time when there was world-wide pressure to reduce restrictions on trade.

Although progress has been made in other areas, it has generally been slower and fraught with difficulties. The Common Agricultural Policy, a key condition for French acceptance of the treaty, has been agreed and is working, but it has been widely criticized both inside and outside the EEC and there are grave doubts as to whether it will be capable of creating the right climate for promoting the much-needed modernization of the European agricultural industry (see Chapter 8). On several occasions disputes over agriculture have brought the Community to the brink of collapse. In the mid-1960s lack of agreement on agricultural policies was a major element in France's quarrel with the other partners and, for a time in 1966, the disagreement brought virtually all the work of the Community to a halt. More recently renegotiation of the Common Agricultural Policy proved to be one of the most difficult issues, when Denmark, Eire and the United Kingdom acceded to the Treaty of Rome. At least, however, there is a common policy for agriculture, but in other areas, notably transport, it has so far proved impossible to harmonize the various national policies into a single EEC policy.

The effective association of overseas territories has also proved to be a somewhat elusive goal. The general principles set out in the treaty itself plan a broad strategy for the first five years to the end of 1962. It was to be a transitional period at the end of which all exports from the associated territories would be able to enter the EEC countries without restriction and imports from the Six would be accorded the same preferential treatment previously enjoyed only by the mother country. A Development Fund was set up to supplement investment programmes already in progress and, over the first five years nearly 600 million units of account were contributed, mostly from France and Germany.[6] Virtually all the investment went to the former French colonies in Africa, two-thirds of the money being spent on economic development and the rest on improving social structure.

These initial arrangements were only ever intended to be temporary and a new agreement was negotiated in 1963 and signed at Yaoundé in Cameroon. Seventeen African states and what is now the Malagasy Republic (Figure 15) were included in the Yaoundé Convention; it embraced a population of nearly seventeen million and ran for five years, from 1964 to 1969. The size of the Development Fund was also increased to 620 million units of account. When this second agreement expired, the convention was again renewed up to 1975 and the Development Fund further increased to 918 million units of account. Provision was also made for formal political institutions in the form

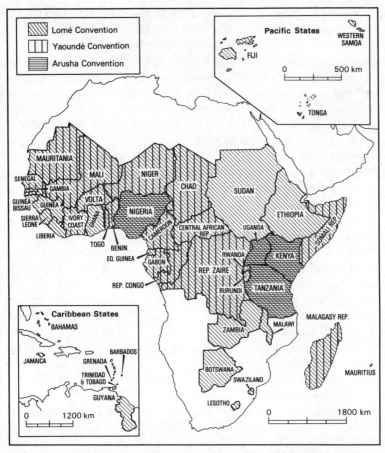

Figure 15   Membership of the Yaoundé, Arusha and Lomé Conventions 1977

of the Council of the Association, the Parliamentary Conference and the Court of Arbitration, on all of which the EEC and the associated states were equally represented. With these developments the association in theory began to assume a more permanent character, but so far the institutional changes have had little practical effect.

Although the agreements were popular with both sides, in reality the impact of these initiatives was relatively paltry. The size of the Development Fund remained small in relation to the overall size of the Community budget. There was also excessive bureaucratic delay in allocating and spending the available funds, so that some money remained unspent at the end of each period. Moves to extend the associate status to other developing countries also met with limited success. An agreement with Nigeria was signed in 1966, after nearly three years of negotiation, but two of the EEC member governments failed to ratify it and the whole approach was dropped. Negotiations between the Community and Kenya, Tanzania and Uganda broke down for similar reasons. Eventually in 1968 the Arusha Convention, embracing all four countries, was signed and ratified and ran in parallel with the second Yaoundé Convention. Despite these developments the sum of the EEC's contribution to the Third World was still small. The organization's main consideration was its domestic economy, and persistent charges of parochialism and a widespread belief that the EEC would never be anything other than a rich man's club were not seriously challenged until the membership was expanded in 1972.

The accession of the United Kingdom to the Treaty of Rome fundamentally altered the relationship between the Community and the developing world. Not only were its overseas dependencies much more extensive than those of any of the other members, but through the Commonwealth a much larger proportion of its trade had traditionally been outside Europe. Links with developing countries in Africa, the Caribbean and the southern Pacific were particularly close. Many of these ties were incompatible with the terms of the Treaty of Rome. It was therefore a precondition of United Kingdom entry that arrangements be made to overcome the immediate effects of the new alliance, as part of a transitional phase, before the United Kingdom became fully integrated into the Community. Foremost among these problems was the plight of the sugar producing countries in the Caribbean, which had hitherto enjoyed unrestricted access to the United Kingdom market. The original six EEC members were also large sugar producers and they looked upon the three newcomers as welcome additions to their market. Tedious as such problems were when the negotiations were actually taking place, they were never really a serious threat to the final success of the United Kingdom application. There was, however, a much longer-term problem relating to the Commonwealth and other trade-dependent territories, which required a more far-reaching and permanent settlement. The overseas aid and preferential trade agreements, which the United Kingdom had traditionally extended towards the developing Commonwealth countries now had to be renegotiated within the context of the Community. The Yaoundé and Arusha Conventions were too limited in scope for this purpose and it was agreed, as part of the terms of United Kingdom entry, that when they ceased on 31 January 1975 a completely new agreement would be negotiated.

The result was the Lomé Convention, signed at Lomé, the capital of Togo, on 28 February 1975, between forty-six African and Caribbean states (Figure 15). It was to run, in the first instance, for five years from 1 April 1975, and membership included all the signatories to the former Yaoundé and Arusha Conventions, together with many of the developing countries of the Commonwealth. As with earlier agreements, the main provision was for duty-free imports into the European Community of industrial products from the developing countries. In addition 96 per cent of agricultural products were also to be allowed to come in duty free. Since the Community absorbed some 70 per cent of the exports from the countries concerned, the agreement was of very considerable importance to them, especially as they in their turn were under no obligation to offer the European Community the same terms for its exports to them.

The Lomé Convention is, however, much more than just a trade agreement, giving unrestricted access to imports. It also provides a guaranteed market for many primary products. The European Community has agreed to purchase 1·4 million tonnes of sugar from the developing countries every year at or above a guaranteed minimum price. It has set aside 375 million units of account in a fund to offset any fluctuations in export earnings from tea, coffee, cocoa, cotton, peanuts, coconuts, palm and palm kernel products, leather and hides, timber, bananas, raw sisal and iron ore thus, effectively, providing a safe market for all these products. In addition the direct aid programme has been more than trebled and 3,390 million units of account have been granted over the five years to help expand the industrial base of the developing countries and to improve their physical infrastructure, by financing new roads, schools, hospitals and other public works. To try to ensure that the best is made of all this investment an Industrial Development Centre is to be established, which will promote private investment from the European Community and monitor development programmes to see that they are well-conceived and properly co-ordinated.

Finally, the institutional framework is to be made much more comprehensive than in the earlier agreements. The main decision-making body will be the Council, comprising one member from each of the developing countries and members of the European Community's Council and Commission. This will deal with the general running of the Convention, but in addition there is to be a Committee of Ambassadors and a Consultative Assembly, which will allow more wide-ranging debates about the external relations of the European Community and, in particular, its relations with the developing world.

The Lomé Convention is potentially an extremely important step forward in the foreign relations of the European Community. It provides for a two-way discussion about the future of trade between the industrial and the developing worlds and may, therefore, help to close one of the most damaging of international political and economic rifts. Only time will tell, but, in the meanwhile, it has been generally welcomed for its careful and positive approach to this difficult problem.[7]

In the field of domestic social policy the EEC has only made slow progress. Article 4 of the Treaty of Rome provided for the setting-up of an Economic and Social Committee, with a wide membership drawn from all sections of society and with a duty to advise the Commission on how best to develop a common policy for social welfare and the social services. So far its achievements have been limited and the discrepancies between benefits in the various member countries have been a considerable source of tension and frustration. One particular difficulty has been the level of commuter traffic across national frontiers, especially between the Netherlands and Germany. Many workers have found it possible to enjoy high wages in Germany and attractive social benefits in the Netherlands at the same time.[8] Another intractable problem has been finding ways and means of making national social security benefits freely available to the population of the Community as a whole, irrespective of whether the claimant is a subject of the particular country where the benefit is being claimed. Arguments over these kinds of detailed issues have tended to divert attention from the more general matters of principle.

The most important success in the field of social policy has been the creation of the European Social Fund for helping to retrain and resettle workers, displaced or forced to move as a result of Community policies. However, until recently the scale of its operations was quite small and it suffered from having only limited powers for direct intervention. In the main its resources could only be used at the behest of one of the member governments. Changes were made in 1970 and the role of the Social Fund strengthened. The Commission itself now has the power to call on its resources to help retrain workers, rather than necessarily having to wait for initiatives from individual national governments. It should now play a much more positive role in helping to cushion the effects of uneven industrial investment within the Community. The Commission is also working on a joint Social Action Programme to try to come to grips with the problems of co-ordinating social policies, but so far there has been no tangible evidence of progress.

One of the main difficulties in assessing the impact of EEC policies is deciding to what extent changes would have occurred, whether or not the organization existed. The outstanding example of this dilemma is the provision for free movement of workers within the countries of the Six. Since 1964 it has been illegal to impede the free movement of workers, and certainly the number of foreign workers, particularly in Germany where there were over 4 million *Gastarbeiter* in the peak year of 1973, has increased sharply since 1958. Unfortunately for the EEC, detailed studies have indicated that the Treaty of Rome probably has had almost no effect on the level of mobility.[9] Free movement of manual workers has always been a characteristic of the European labour market and the EEC legislation only served to formalize the *status quo*. There is also no evidence that workers from non-EEC countries have suffered any discrimination since 1958. Spanish labour has continued to move freely into France, and in Germany Greek, Yugoslav and Turkish workers have all been more important than Italians since the mid-1960s. In non-manual jobs the free movement of labour continues to be something of a myth, despite the EEC legislation, because of the reluctance of national governments to validate foreign professional qualifications. This has not only inhibited the movement of the more highly educated and better qualified workers, it has also severely restricted the supposed freedom to offer services throughout the Community, irrespective of country of birth. The difficulties involved in maintaining standards and ensuring equivalence of qualifications between different countries are self-evident, but little real attempt has so far been made to come to terms with the problem.

In the last analysis the most crucial area of disagreement among the Six has been on the subject of monetary union. During the latter half of the 1960s the system of exchange rates varying within fixed limits, developed under the OEEC, began to break down and be replaced by a system of floating rates. Under the new system currencies were allowed to find their own value against each other, rather than the rates being fixed. The effect was to allow each member government in the EEC the freedom to determine the value of its currency on international money markets, and it gave them a strong lever for controlling the effects of Community policies domestically through exchange rates. It is a ploy that has been widely used, despite several attempts to try to work out an agreed common monetary policy. In theory it was agreed in 1972 that fixed exchange rates or a common currency should operate from 1980, but preparations for this considerable development in Community co-operation have been slow so far and there seems little likelihood of the target date being met. Meanwhile the floating rates continue to undermine the effectiveness of budgetary decisions and common policies in the Community.

The institutions which governed and ran the EEC were very similar to those already developed for the ECSC. The main executive organ was the nine (now thirteen) man Commission located in Brussels, which was responsible for formulating and executing policy. The Commission was answerable to the Council of Ministers, made up of Ministers from the member states, which acted as the main channel of communication between the EEC and national governments. To a lesser extent the Commission was also responsible to the European Parliament in Strasbourg. When the Treaty of Rome was signed, it was decided to merge the ECSC Common Assembly into a new European Parliament, acting for both organizations as well as for Euratom. The 142 members (now 198) were empowered to receive reports from the Commission and, by a two-thirds majority, they could censure its actions. Similarly a single Court of Justice, sitting in Luxembourg also served all three communities. The Court was to ensure that the provisions of the treaties were properly implemented and carried out and to adjudicate between member states in grievances arising from the operation of the treaties. The only truly new institution established by the Treaty of Rome was the advisory Economic and Social Committee (see above, page 100).

The European Atomic Energy Community (Euratom)

The European Atomic Energy Community, universally known as Euratom, came into existence on 1 January 1958 under the terms of a second Treaty of Rome. Without question it has been the least active and successful of the three communities, mainly because it failed to anticipate correctly the relative importance of nuclear energy in Europe's energy budget in the 1960s. In 1956 nuclear power seemed destined to be the main energy source of the immediate future and, as a result of its military history, there was widespread concern that its development should be placed under some form of international control. Euratom was to be the European equivalent of the Nuclear Energy Agency of the OECD. In the event nuclear power was rapidly overshadowed by oil after 1958 and, even now, it is still only a minor source of energy in Europe. Not only is nuclear energy in general more costly to produce than electricity from oil, it has also proved much more difficult than expected to develop a sufficiently safe technology for coping with the environmental and health risks.

One of the most interesting features of Euratom when it was set up was its projected future as the spearhead of a common energy policy in the Community. However, as the importance of nuclear energy faded, so did talk of a common energy policy. The shelving of this key proposal occasioned little comment, until the rapid rise in the cost of crude oil threatened the stability of all the western industrial economies in the mid-1970s. Then the lack of forward planning in the Community was sharply criticized and the failure to agree a common energy policy cited as one of the chief underlying causes of the ensuing world recession. There is still nothing that could be called a common energy policy in western Europe. The only tangible progress made since 1958 was when the three communities were merged in 1967 and the fragmentation of responsibility – ECSC for coal, EEC for oil and gas, Euratom for nuclear energy – was reduced, if not removed.

The institutions of Euratom were almost identical to those of the EEC, except that the Euratom Commission had five members instead of nine. The Court of Justice and the European Parliament were shared with the ECSC and the EEC and Euratom also had joint access with the EEC to the Economic and Social Committee.

Adapting the European Communities

Despite the strict guidelines laid down in their treaties of incorporation, the three communities were never static. Each adapted to conditions as it found them and tried to react positively to political, economic and social initiatives, both from member states and from third parties. As a result all three organizations have evolved over the years, changing their character quite considerably in the process. Several references have already been made to the progressive integration of the ECSC, the EEC and Euratom, which culminated in 1967 with the creation of a single European Community, run by the permanent Commission in Brussels, the European Parliament in Strasbourg and the European Court of Justice in Luxembourg. It was a development which had been planned from the moment the three communities had been founded and, when the time came to give effect to the merger the only real difficulties were questions of detail, such as which city should house which institution.

A much thornier problem was whether or not to extend Community membership to other European countries and the form that membership should take. The United Kingdom refusal to join first the ECSC and later the EEC and Euratom was a serious setback to the European movement, but, in the eyes of some members of the Six, a temporary one. Behind the scenes future United Kingdom participation was actively encouraged and, in 1960, the United Kingdom government put out the first tentative feelers about membership. In 1961 a formal application was made to join all three communities. Denmark and Eire quickly followed suit and also applied for full membership, as did Norway in the following year. In addition a new category of member was created when Greece was granted associate member status in 1961. Associate membership brought with it few privileges, but, in Greece's case, was tantamount to a declaration of intent that it would become a full member of the Community once its economy was sufficiently developed to be able to withstand full integration with the major industrial economies of western Europe. A similar understanding was negotiated with Turkey in 1963. In 1961 another group of European countries tried to use the associate member status to gain access to the economic advantages of EEC membership, without having to embrace the political implications of the Treaty of Rome. Austria, Switzerland and Sweden were all members of EFTA (see Chapter 6) and politically neutral. On the one hand they doubted whether EFTA had a long-term future, but they were prevented by their neutrality from applying for full EEC membership. After some discussion the Community turned down these overtures and similar ones from Spain in 1962, indicating clearly that it was only interested in wholehearted commitment to the Community.

Ten full members, plus up to six associate members, would clearly have radically altered the whole basis of the European Community. In retrospect it is clear that in 1961 the organization was not internally strong enough to manage such a major upheaval and, even though negotiations dragged on until 1963, when the French President, De Gaulle, finally exercised his veto, ruling out any possibility of enlargement in the short-term, there was considerable relief all round. Nevertheless the other five members were exceedingly annoyed that the only outcome of two whole years of negotiation was the addition of two associate members to the organization.

In May 1967 the United Kingdom made a rather half-hearted second attempt to join, but hopes were never very high on either side and, after six months, De Gaulle again exercised his right of veto. Really serious negotiations were virtually impossible so long as he remained President of France, for he was opposed in principle to United Kingdom membership. He firmly believed that it would alter the whole direction and balance of power in the Community to the detriment of France. However, once De Gaulle retired in 1969 the Six almost immediately made overtures to reopen the issue and formal applications were made by the United Kingdom, Denmark, Eire and Norway.

The problems posed by the prospective enlargement were in many respects similar to those surrounding the original negotiations leading up to the signing of the Treaty of Rome. The United Kingdom's relationship with its Commonwealth had to be safeguarded and transitional arrangements made for phasing out traditional trade agreements, in particular those relating to dairy products from New Zealand and sugar from the West Indies, both of which were contrary to the Community's Common Agricultural Policy. Internally the quite different systems of agricultural subsidy in the four applicant countries had to be smoothly integrated with the Community policy as well. The reserve status of the £ sterling had to be agreed. An acceptable arrangement with those EFTA countries not wishing to join the Community as full members had to be worked out. Finally the common fisheries policy agreed by the Six, giving free access to all fishing grounds under their jurisdiction, had to be modified so as to protect the large United Kingdom and Norwegian industries. All were problems that could only be solved by compromise on both sides and this time there was a genuine will to succeed. Eventually all four countries signed the treaty of accession on 22 January 1972, with effect from 1 January 1973. Prior to that date, Norway in fact abandoned its application under strong domestic pressure before the treaty actually came into effect. The fishing and agricultural lobbies felt that their interests had been poorly looked after in the negotiations on entry and, after a referendum, the Norwegian government withdrew.

Expanding the membership of the Community to nine was a change of such magnitude that it was almost inevitable that the basic aims and objectives would have to be redefined to take account of the new interests. A Summit Conference was convened in October 1972 to chart the progress of the organization for the next decade. The final communiqué revealed some important changes, reflecting the different interest of all the new members and the United Kingdom in particular.[10] The central importance of economic union was reaffirmed, but went further, in that 31 December 1980 was set as the deadline for achieving full economic and monetary union. An essential prerequisite of this development was thought to be a fully-fledged regional policy, which would allow regional imbalances in the Community's economy to be corrected. It was agreed that a centrally administered Regional Development Fund had to be established before the end of 1973, as a first step towards ironing out these inequalities. The social policy was to be strengthened and common policies for science and technology, the environment and energy were to receive special priority. Finally there was a call to strengthen the Community's institutions, especially the somewhat moribund European Parliament. By doing so it was hoped that the European Community would come to play an independent role as the spokesman for all the nine members on world affairs. The ultimate objective remained as it had been ever since 1948, full European union.

Subsequent progress has been slow, hampered by the world recession and by further doubts about continuing United Kingdom membership, which were only finally dispelled after the overwhelming vote of confidence in the national referendum in June 1975. Economic and monetary union certainly seem no closer and, as yet, there are few tangible results from the Social Action Programme announced in 1973. The only important new development has been the Regional Development Fund, unveiled in May 1973. Potentially it could be a powerful instrument for countering the disequilibria inherent in the regional economic structure of the Community (see Chapter 8), but as yet it is too early to pass final judgement. The situation is symptomatic of the state of the Community as a whole: the structure exists, but the commitment of member governments is not total. The conflict between national loyalties and the greater good of a single supranational European Community remains unresolved. A period of political stability and social and economic consolidation are needed to allow the organization to establish its own role. It is very much open to question, whether such a breathing-space will be forthcoming. Agreement has now been reached in principle on Greece's accession to the Community and Portugal is also expected to be admitted soon. An undetermined application from Spain is still pending. If any of these countries do become full members, it will significantly broaden the range of economic and social problems with which the European Community has to deal and inevitably alter the nature of the organization itself.

6

The European Free Trade Association: An Apolitical Approach to Integration

The Development of EFTA

The members of the European Free Trade Association (EFTA) are a group of countries which came together with the limited, but clearly defined objective of creating a free trade area for industrial goods. The association is a loose one and, since it was formed in 1960, has included as many as nine European countries and as few as seven. The present members are Austria, Iceland, Norway, Portugal, Switzerland and Sweden, with Finland an associate member, but in the 1960s, when the association was in its heyday, the United Kingdom and Denmark were also members and the EFTA market included more than 100 million people (Figure 16).

Although in a strict legal sense EFTA is completely independent of the EEC, in practice its development has always been tied closely to the European Community. The origin of the association was very much a reaction to the signing of the Treaty of Rome by the six original members of the EEC and EFTA's form and aims are a clear refutation of the Community's approach to integration: there is no treaty of incorporation, and integration is to be achieved through a free trade area rather than a customs union. Although the initial conception was in many ways somewhat *ad hoc*, EFTA's economic success gained the association a considerable reputation, enhancing not only its economic stature, but its political influence as well. Despite the fact that formal political institutions had been intentionally eschewed, the association was an economic force to be reckoned with, and this gave it considerable bargaining power, especially in relations with the EEC. EFTA illustrated that there was more than one way of achieving closer economic integration and that certainly

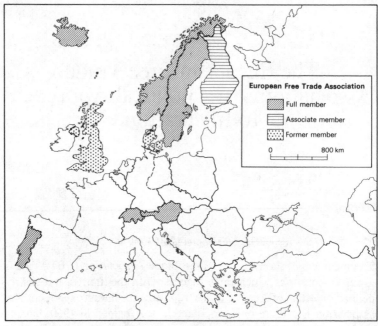

Figure 16   Membership of the European Free Trade Association 1977

there was no absolute need to go through all the formal and difficult procedures of creating a customs union.

The early political manoeuvrings, which eventually led to the establishment of EFTA, were all part of the much more general discussion going on in western Europe during the latter half of the 1950s, about the future of the OEEC and the institutions that should succeed it. The European Community was unacceptable to the majority of OEEC members for a variety of political and economic reasons. Some were barred from signing a treaty with such supranational connotations by virtue of their constitutions; others were too weak economically to contemplate entering into a customs union (on an equal footing) with the major European industrial nations; still others were unwilling to renounce existing trade commitments to non-European countries. The United Kingdom took the lead in opposing the proposed European Economic Community, and in 1958, the United Kingdom government initiated a series of negotiations to try to persuade the six members of the EEC to participate in a much wider free trade area restricted to industrial goods. The approach failed, mainly because at that time the EEC wanted to consolidate its own position, rather than extend the scope of the organization, but there was also considerable scepticism about the effectiveness of such a limited venture as a free trade area.

Once the United Kingdom overtures had been finally rejected towards the end of 1958, the non-EEC members of the OEEC were forced to reconsider their position. Four of them, Greece, Iceland, Eire and Turkey were prepared to let the whole matter drop, at least for the time being, mainly because none of them had economies which were sufficiently developed and diversified to benefit immediately from free trade in industrial goods. The other seven, Austria, Denmark, Norway, Portugal, Sweden, Switzerland and the United Kingdom, decided to press ahead on their own. The advantages of a more liberalized system of trade were apparent to them from the achievements of the OEEC, but they realized, as Meyer has noted so perceptively, that: 'In order to get on well with one's neighbours, it is not necessary to do things in common with them, but it is essential not to irritate them.'[1] A free trade area fulfils both these requirements: it exempts the constituent countries from all restrictions on trade, such as import duties, export subsidies and quota restrictions, but allows them to retain their own external tariffs towards non-member countries and their own internal direct tax structures and social services. Such an approach was particularly attractive to the United Kingdom, since it was similar in many important respects to the relationship it had evolved with the Commonwealth. The analogy is once again clearly explained by Meyer:

> The Commonwealth type of approach builds on what there is. Existing states are taken for granted. Ways and means are being sought to improve the international behaviour between states. But it is better behaviour that is wanted not better states. It is good behaviour not to annoy. The most likely cause of annoyance within a group such as the Seven lies in economic divisions that deny equal access to economic opportunities. Free trade between the citizens of these states gives regionals the same economic opportunities as nationals enjoy. Hence regionals get the maximum economic opportunities the region can offer.[2]

The United Kingdom's enthusiasm for the free trade area approach was crucial, since its population of 54 million comprised more than half the total potential market and it therefore was bound to dominate any serious negotiations. Once the decision had been taken to try to form a European free trade area outside the EEC, progress was rapid. After little more than a year of negotiation EFTA existed, established under the terms of the Stockholm Convention on 4 January 1960. All restrictions on trade in industrial goods were to be removed in a series of predetermined stages with complete abolition by 1 January 1970.

The only exception was Portugal, which because of its relatively under-developed economy was to be allowed to retain certain restrictions until 1 January 1980. Incidentally it was also tacitly recognized by all the signatories, that EFTA would perform the role of keeping them together as a coherent group, while they tried to negotiate a satisfactory arrangement with the EEC, either singly or as a group.

The administrative flexibility of the EFTA agreement in comparison with the Treaty of Rome was underlined almost as soon as the Stockholm Convention had been signed. Finland had strong traditional trading links with all the Scandinavian countries, especially Sweden, but treaty obligations to the Soviet Union prevented it from becoming a full member of EFTA. However in 1961 Finland was made an associate member of the association, which allowed full participation in the working of the free trade area, without having to formally embrace the Convention. Such an arrangement would have been impossible within the EEC and emphasized how unimportant centralized, supranational institutions were in EFTA. To all intents and purposes the association had gained a new member, but with the minimum of administrative fuss.

Although EFTA proved to be assiduous and successful in pursuing its free trade objectives, the desire of all the members to ultimately achieve a working relationship with the EEC, gave the association an air of impermanence and was a continual source of tension and mutual suspicion. In the summer of 1961, little more than a year after EFTA had come into operation, the United Kingdom decided to apply for membership of the EEC. The other members felt that the association could not work without the United Kingdom, so they too either applied for full membership (Denmark and Norway) or associate status. There then followed a hiatus of nearly eighteen months while the applications were considered, before General De Gaulle vetoed British entry. The rejection gave new impetus to EFTA and the members decided to try to speed up the reduction in tariffs and subsidies and the abolition of quotas, so as to make the free trade area fully operative from 1967 rather than 1970.

In October 1964 EFTA was again thrown into a state of chaos, this time by the United Kingdom's unilateral introduction of a 15 per cent surcharge on a wide range of industrial imports. The action was taken to safeguard the United Kingdom's balance of payments and, if the other members had been consulted in advance, the surcharge could have been agreed to as an emergency measure under the terms of the Convention. Their complaint was at the lack of prior notice, which clearly violated the requirements of the Convention. The surcharge was in operation for just over two years until November 1966 and, although it did not fundamentally impair progress towards the free trade area, it further undermined confidence in the long term viability of EFTA as a whole.

Almost inevitably there were repercussions. It was generally agreed that the association could not survive without the United Kingdom as a member and, while its commitment was in doubt, there was a natural tendency for other members to play safe and negotiate alternative arrangements. Austria took the most active steps in this direction, when it reopened discussions with the EEC in 1963 about the possibility of being admitted to associate status. Talks dragged on for over three years, but with little enthusiasm on the part of the EEC Commission, who saw such an enlargement of the Community as potentially weakening the organization's internal cohesion. Towards the end of 1966 the matter was quietly dropped.

Whatever the doubts among EFTA members, the success of the association in creating a free trade area and the increase in trade that ensued was a source of envy to those countries that had decided neither to join EFTA nor the EEC. In 1967 Eire flirted briefly with the United Kingdom over the possibility of setting up a separate free trade area between the two countries, but in the end nothing was agreed. Yugoslavia began conversations with EFTA in 1965 about the possibility of establishing a working relationship and, even though nothing positive emerged, it was yet another indication of the interest and envy that the association's success aroused. In Yugoslavia's case the stumbling block in the way of progress was the virtual impossibility of making a centrally planned economy compatible with the principles of free trade. The next approach to EFTA came from Iceland in November 1968 and this time talks bore fruit and the association formally welcomed its ninth member on 1 March 1970.

Within EFTA itself however the doubts continued and in the spring of 1967 the United Kingdom decided once more to apply for membership of the EEC. Once again the association was thrown into a state of uncertainty and, even though the second application was rejected as firmly as the first by the French, it was clear to all that the United Kingdom intended placing its long-term hopes on the EEC, rather than EFTA. Once General De Gaulle had been succeeded as President of France by Georges Pompidou, it was generally accepted that it was only a matter of time until the United Kingdom renewed its membership application and that this time it would be successful. Negotiations were eventually completed on 22 January 1972, when the United Kingdom and Denmark signed the Treaty of Rome, together with Eire. Overnight EFTA was robbed of nearly 60 million people and its market was reduced by nearly two-thirds. If it had not been for the rejection of EEC membership by a last minute referendum in Norway the reduction would have been even more severe.

In one respect however the accession of the United Kingdom and Denmark to the Treaty of Rome allowed EFTA to considerably further its own ambitions. From the outset there had been those who had primarily viewed the association as a ploy for achieving a free trade area covering the whole of western Europe. One of the concessions which the United Kingdom and Denmark were able to extract from the EEC when they joined, was the promise of associate status for the rest of their partners in EFTA. Agreements were signed by the EEC with all six remaining members, guaranteeing steady progress by a series of predetermined stages towards free trade in industrial goods by 1 July 1977. In effect this will mean that the free trade area, covering all the former European members of the OEEC will eventually become a reality. That this has been allowed to happen is due almost entirely to the success of EFTA during the 1960s, which dispelled any doubts about the possibility of organizing a free trade area among such a politically and economically diverse group of states.

The Stockholm Convention

The Stockholm Convention is a quite different type of agreement to the formal treaties establishing the European Communities. It is essentially a voluntary association, free to welcome new members at any time and one from which existing members may withdraw, without theoretically causing fundamental damage either to EFTA, or to themselves. The only restriction is a proviso that any member wishing to withdraw must give twelve months' notice. The terms of the Convention itself are also extremely flexible. There is specific provision in the agreement for continuous assessment and review and the whole document may be revised and rewritten, if and when the members deem it desirable.

Nonetheless the basic objectives of EFTA, as set out in Article 2 of the Convention, are clear and unequivocal and have not been revised since the association was inaugurated in 1960. The primary purpose is to promote conditions, which will lead to sustained economic growth in all the member countries, while at the same time guarding against unemployment, inflation and the squandering of resources. The means for achieving these unexceptionable ends are free trade between the member states and support for all moves to remove trade barriers in the world in general. In practice this called for a phased programme to reduce tariffs and abolish quotas on trade in non-agricultural goods between members of the association. Initially the target date for complete abolition of all these restrictions was 1 January 1970, but it soon became clear that progress could be much more rapid and a revised timetable was introduced. Import duties were reduced by fixed percentages across the board, starting with a 20 per cent reduction on 1 July 1960, leading to final removal on 31 December 1966. A parallel programme was carried out to remove all import quotas. The only levy on imports which any member could legitimately impose after the beginning of 1967 was revenue duty. This is a non-discriminatory tax, which a country imposes on a particular range of goods, irrespective of whether they are domestically produced or imported. If, however, the country does not produce that particular product itself, the tax amounts to an import duty. The only case where this became an issue in EFTA was Norway's refusal to reduce tariffs on motor cars. This caused some resentment in the United Kingdom and Sweden with their large car industries, but the Norwegian market was relatively so small that it never posed a major problem. In general revenue duty has not been used to any significant extent to distort the overall free trade objectives of EFTA.

The only member countries not subject to the full weight of these rules are Portugal and Iceland. Both have relatively underdeveloped economies and their partners recognized that the Portuguese and Icelandic economies would require special protection to see them through their growth stages. The provisions, worked out in the first instance for Portugal alone, basically extend the transition period for the removal of import duties and quota restrictions up until 1980, although the exemption only applies to industries exporting less than 15 per cent of their output. The Portuguese government is also further encouraged to keep the number of protected industries to a minimum, by a special clause which allows it to remove exemption from any industry it regards as sufficiently developed to withstand the full rigours of competition in the free trade area. The other protective measure open to Portugal is a clause, which allows it to impose quantitative restrictions on the export of any exhaustable mining product, if in their view this is likely to endanger supplies needed for domestic industries. By and large similar concessions have been granted to Iceland, although, until the end of 1973, it enjoyed the additional benefit of being able to impose import quotas as well.

The essence of the Stockholm Convention is to create a free trade area, hemmed in as little as possible by institutions and rules and regulations, but inevitably a minimal structural framework has to be enforced. The main problems arise in dealing with imports from outside EFTA. Although one of the express aims of the association is to avoid the creation of a customs union with a common external tariff as such, differential policies on imports of raw materials and semi-manufactured goods can eventually lead to unfair trade advantages being conferred on some member countries. It was this difficulty which made necessary the crucial Rules of Origin. A means had to be found of restricting the free trade to products manufactured within EFTA, otherwise importers from outside would simply channel their goods through the member country with the lowest tariff and use it as a staging post for flooding the markets in all the others. Two strategies were devised to deal with this situation. An exporter had to show, either that at least 50 per cent of the value of his product had been added to it within EFTA, or that it had undergone a specified number and types of manufacturing process, so that the original raw materials were now an integral part of a completely new product. If one of these conditions were not satisfied then the product was not eligible for free trade status within EFTA. Although on the face of it the procedures would seem to be complex and cumbersome to operate, in practice they have worked well. All exporters sign Declarations of Origin and spot checks to prevent abuse are made at ports of entry by customs officials who have the power to deal directly with any irregularities. There has never been a single instance when the central EFTA Council has had a case against the violation of the Rules of Origin.

Another difficulty facing the EFTA Council, in its attempt to guarantee the operation of a free trade system among the member countries, was to establish effective rules of competition. There are many ways of tinkering with the operation of a free market, some of them difficult to detect and even more difficult to control. The Stockholm Convention identified three major areas where legislation was felt to be necessary. First of all government subsidies and quota restrictions on exports had to be removed. This was the first positive step taken jointly by the EFTA members, who agreed to abandon all such preferential measures by the end of 1961. Unfortunately, however, the same preferred status could be achieved in other less direct ways and these too had to be eliminated. The most damaging was the system known as 'drawback', whereby raw materials were effectively permitted to enter a country duty free because certain manufacturers were able to claim a rebate from the government in respect of the import duty. The practice was widespread in Europe and it took some time to phase it out. Eventually the last vestiges of it were removed when all other import controls came to an end at the beginning of 1967. The other area of governmental activity which required strict surveillance was the nationalized industries, many of which did not operate strictly according to commercial principles. This problem was particularly prominent in the United Kingdom where both the steel and coal industries were nationalized.

Other threats to free competition were more obvious and therefore easier to control. Monopolies and market sharing and price fixing between large companies had to be guarded against and all member governments had powers to ban such practices once their use could be proved. The remaining significant restrictive practices were mainly limitations on the freedom of firms to extend their manufacturing operations from their country of origin to the territory of other members of the free trade area, and the non-transferability of professional qualifications. In neither instance however is there any evidence that these curbs significantly impaired EFTA's operations.

The free trade area established by EFTA specifically excluded agricultural products and foodstuffs, because, like the EEC, the association recognized that the agricultural market was so heavily influenced by government subsidies in every conceivable way, that it would be impossible to make it part of a free trade system. At the same time the distinction between agricultural products and those from other industries is by no means always clear, so that crops and animal products could not be ignored completely. Under the Stockholm Convention two methods are used to improve trading conditions in the agricultural sector. First, there is a list, which is kept as short as possible, of those products to be excluded from free trade. Since the list is the subject of negotiation between member countries, what is included or excluded is not always strictly logical, but on the whole processed foods are treated as industrial products and all others exempted. The other method is a series of bilateral treaties between individual member governments. This option would of course be open whether or not EFTA existed, but there is a widespread belief that the spirit of co-operation and the frequent high level contacts, produced by participation in EFTA, have had the effect of making such bilateral agreements easier to negotiate.

One of the distinguishing features of EFTA, as an organization is the absence of centralized institutions and supranational control. The association's only permanent statutory body is the Council, operating at ministerial level. It is the policy-making body, deciding the broad

objectives of EFTA, and it has no powers or machinery for implementing decisions. That is left entirely to the individual member
governments. Even when there is a dispute between two states affecting the Convention and the Council upholds a protest, its only sanction is to empower the aggrieved party to take retaliatory action, by
suspending the free trade benefits conferred by EFTA. This was all it
was able to do when the United Kingdom unilaterally and quite
wrongly imposed its 15 per cent import surcharge in 1964. In general
however such indirect sanctions are of minor importance and
only underline the fact that the Stockholm Convention depends for
its successful operation on the good will and co-operation of its
members.

Nevertheless, despite the absence of a central bureaucratic core,
over the years the Council has spawned several sub-committees. As
early as 1960 the Consultative Committee was established, consisting
of representatives of the main sectors of economic life in each of the
member countries, including the trade unions, in order to promote
co-operation and co-ordination of general economic policies. In 1966
this committee in turn set up an Economic and Social Sub-Committee
to examine and make recommendations on economic and social
problems, resulting from the process of economic integration set in
motion by EFTA. In 1963 the Council created the Economic Development Committee, to advise member states on ways of improving the
structure of their economies. Portugal, in particular, made use of this
facility, calling on the economic expertise of its more industrially
advanced partners to help develop its own economy. From time to
time there have also been other specialist working parties, set up to
examine specific problems arising from the growth of the free trade
area. Yet even taking these new bodies into account, EFTA has never
seriously attempted to develop a separate identity and existence from
that of its members. The Stockholm Convention is a declaration of
intent free of institutions and self-perpetuating bureaucracy.

The structure partly reflected a genuine belief on the part of the
EFTA members that there should be a minimum of new institutions,
but there was also a strong element of political realism in their
position. Most regarded the Stockholm Convention as merely a stage
in the progress towards attaining a free trade area covering the whole
of western Europe; they did not want to create any institution that
could conceivably impede the achievement of that concept in the
future. However, when Denmark and the United Kingdom transferred
their allegiance from the Stockholm Convention to the Treaty of
Rome in 1972, there could be no question of the other EFTA members

coming to an arrangement with the European Community as a bloc. The links between them were too tenuous. For this reason separate trade agreements were negotiated between the Community and each EFTA country individually. Although they were all virtually identical, the approach underlined the fundamental purpose of a free trade area. It exists to promote trade between its members and intentionally refrains from any interference in their policies towards third parties. The agreements with the European Community adhered strictly to this policy.

The Members

The membership of EFTA is quite different from any of the other major European organizations. Physically the countries are widely dispersed around the periphery of western Europe and the lack of contiguity makes integration on the scale envisaged by the European Community both unlikely and, in the eyes of many of the member governments, politically undesirable. There is also a considerable diversity of political philosophy, and little enthusiasm for developing common policies, other than in strictly economic matters. Finally, variations in the level of economic development and in the nature of the constituent economies, have produced a situation where each country has had to face very different problems and derive quite different benefits from membership. The strongest link between the members of EFTA has always been a shared belief in the efficacy of free trade for stimulating economic activity and growth. For all these reasons it is somewhat unrealistic to consider the countries as a group: each signed the Stockholm Convention determined, for one reason or another, to preserve its identity and determined to avoid becoming submerged in a supranational organization.

Austria

Austria with a population of 7·4 million and an area of 83,849 square kilometres is one of the smaller countries of western Europe and has had to struggle hard to preserve its independence and separate political identity throughout most of the twentieth century. For ten years after the end of the Second World War it was occupied by the Allies and administered under four-power control. The price of eventual independence was a guarantee that permanent neutrality would be the cornerstone of the nation's foreign policy. It was a stance which ruled out any possibility of joining the European Community, because of the political implications of the Treaty of Rome. Despite the fact that

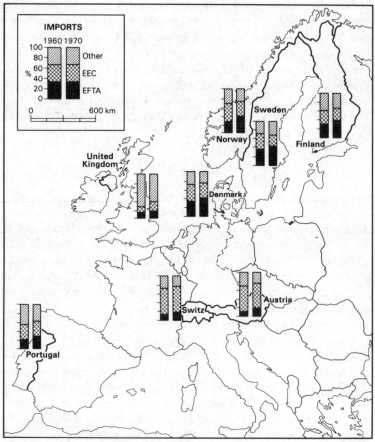

Figure 17   Changes in the pattern of imports in the member countries of the
European Free Trade Association 1960–70

the bulk of Austria's foreign trade was with the six EEC countries,
West Germany in particular (Figures 17 and 18), it was forced, somewhat against its will, to look elsewhere for economic allies. From the
start, therefore, it participated, somewhat reluctantly, in EFTA. Probably more than any of the other members, Austria tended to view the
association simply as a ploy for achieving an all-inclusive west
European free trade area. Physical remoteness from most of the other
members of the association tended to reinforce the basic reservations.
Traditionally Austria's links had all been with the German-speaking
countries of Europe, but, after signing the Stockholm Convention, it
suddenly found itself thrust into an economic alliance, dominated by

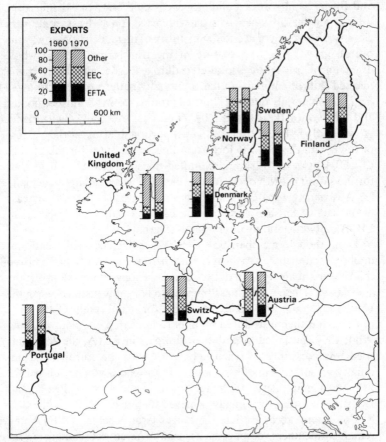

Figure 18   Changes in the pattern of exports in the member countries of the
European Free Trade Association 1960–70

the United Kingdom and, to a lesser extent, Scandinavia. It was a
change which was bound to require a fundamental reorientation in
the country's whole approach to international affairs.

After becoming a member of EFTA in 1960, the Austrian economy
began to expand rapidly, although it is impossible to say to what
extent the growth was attributable directly to membership of the free
trade area. Between 1960 and 1970 imports increased over 200 per
cent from 1,144 to 3,549 million US dollars and exports nearly
300 per cent from $US965 to 2,857 million. The general expansion in
the level of trade raised economic standards and reduced the disparities between Austria and its richer neighbours – West Germany

and Switzerland – to a point where it could be claimed that: 'the time is not far off when Austria will reach, or at least come very close to, the degree of economic maturity of its models'.[3] Nor was the overall growth the only feature of the transformation, the whole direction of trade was also altered during the decade. There was a marked shift of emphasis in the commodity pattern of exports, away from raw materials and semi-finished products towards finished goods, and trade with the other EFTA countries, especially Switzerland, grew rapidly in both absolute and proportional terms, at the expense of trade with the EEC. Before according all the glory for this change to EFTA however, it should be noted that one of the main reasons for the slower growth of trade with the EEC was a fall in the demand for Austrian raw materials and semi-finished products. The increase in the sale of finished goods to the EEC was almost as great as to EFTA, notwithstanding the common external tariff.

Even though membership of EFTA coincided with, and undoubtedly contributed to the most prosperous era Austria had enjoyed this century, it always had doubts about the long-term viability of the association. These misgivings appeared to be amply justified, when the United Kingdom first decided to apply for membership of the EEC in 1961, and then introduced an import surcharge on goods in 1964. While they continued to play their full part in EFTA, the Austrians tried unsuccessfully to reach agreement with the European Community on some form of association. In the end it was not until 1972 with the signing of the trade agreement in the wake of British and Danish entry, that they finally achieved their goal. By that time they had also come to appreciate the longer-term benefits of EFTA and remained members, despite the association's reduced circumstances.

Switzerland

Political neutrality was as important to Switzerland as it was to Austria, but in this case the policy was not a recent precondition of independence, but an essential part of the life of the nation. Switzerland has existed as a separate entity in Europe since the fourteenth century, but in spite of its long history, it has never represented a single cultural tradition. The country was born as a federation and has firmly remained one, with each of the cantons playing its own part on an equal basis with all the others in the government of the nation. Frequently a balance has been hard to sustain and neutrality 'avoids the necessity of having to take political positions which could be the source of internal tensions between political parties or even between different sections of the population and provides for the peaceful existence of peoples with different languages, religions and traditions within a single state'.[4] The arguments against Switzerland joining the European Community were therefore even stronger than those ranged against Austria, but attractions of EFTA were greater. The Swiss were a traditional trading nation and any moves to reduce trade barriers were welcome, so long as they did not involve loss of sovereignty to a supranational authority. In addition to the political pressures, there were good economic reasons why a free trade area in industrial goods suited Switzerland better than an all-embracing common market. As in nearly every other west European country agriculture is protected by a cocoon of tariffs, variable quotas, government subsidies and high consumer prices, but in Switzerland the extent of the protection is greater than anywhere else. Prices in general are above EEC levels, and productivity and farm incomes are very high. Although the agricultural labour force is small, it satisfies nearly 60 per cent of domestic needs. The Swiss were naturally loathe to interfere with this delicate balance and saw in EFTA a means of achieving enhanced free trade without infringing their extensive system of agricultural protection.

Between 1960 and 1970 the volume of Swiss trade grew rapidly, especially with its EFTA partners (Figures 17 and 18). Austria and the United Kingdom were the two countries where the increase was most marked, although there were absolute and relative gains both in imports and exports with all the members. An important aspect of the new trade was the way it diversified. Largely as a result of the contacts achieved through EFTA, the Swiss were able to sell completely new ranges of products, particularly in the United Kingdom. Swiss furniture sales, for instance, grew rapidly throughout the 1960s. Nevertheless these successes should not be allowed to disguise the true balance of Swiss trade, which was and remains strongly orientated towards the EEC countries. West Germany, France and Italy have accounted for well over 50 per cent of Swiss trade since the end of the Second World War and show no real sign of relaxing their grip, despite the emergence of attractive new markets in EFTA.

Sweden

Sweden is another of the EFTA members that adheres to a policy of strict political neutrality, but, in this case, it was only a contributory cause of the general lack of enthusiasm for the aims and objectives of the European Community. Unlike many of its neighbours, Sweden is a large country (411,406 square kilometres) with a small population (8·1 million) and is richly endowed with raw materials. It has the largest forest cover of any European country, either west or east of the Iron Curtain and much of the timber is relatively accessible via the many rivers. In the north there are some of the richest iron ore deposits in the world, as well as smaller quantities of lead, copper, nickel, gold and silver. Finally, abundant hydro-electric power has made Sweden more independent of foreign sources of energy than most other industrial countries. Such a rich endowment of natural resources has made it possible for Sweden to participate competitively in world trade at a number of different levels. Traditionally, it has been primarily a supplier of raw materials and semi-finished products to the old established industrial nations, not only in Europe, but throughout the world. In the long-term, however, the wealth created by this trade also provided the opportunity to diversify the domestic industrial base and now manufacturing is the cornerstone of the economy. The new emphasis has developed new markets: the bulk of Sweden's trade in manufactured goods is with its Scandinavian neighbours, rather than with the United States, the EEC countries, or with the United Kingdom, its main markets for raw materials and semi-finished goods.

Taking the pattern of trade as a whole a number of important points emerge. Historically Sweden was not so closely tied to European markets as most other of its west European neighbours (Figures 17 and 18) and it had strong political reasons for not wanting to alter this situation. The country's neutrality was largely dictated by mistrust of Soviet territorial ambitions on its eastern flank; by extending the lack of commitment from political to economic matters, Sweden has been able to reinforce the genuineness of its independent stance and to dissuade the Soviet government from extending its military control deeper into the Baltic region. The founding of EFTA also helped to further diversify Sweden's commercial links. The close cultural ties with Norway, Finland and Denmark made these countries especially receptive to Swedish manufactures and the abolition of tariffs and quotas under the terms of the Stockholm Convention, simply made access to an already eager market that much easier. The extent of the new trade can be gauged from the fact that, although the combined population of the three countries is only 14 million, they bought nearly a third of Sweden's exports in 1970, the bulk of them manufactured goods. In 1960 it was less than one quarter. From the Swedish point of view, EFTA has consolidated existing close cultural links and confirmed its political independence, most importantly in the eyes of the Soviet Union. It was more than enough to guarantee the country's continuing support for the association, even after the United Kingdom and Denmark left to join the EEC.

Norway

Of all the countries in EFTA Norway has probably benefited least from membership of the association. Although the Norwegian economy has grown rapidly in the past two decades, a relatively small part of the growth has been in manufacturing industry. Service industries and especially merchant shipping dominate the economy. In 1970, shipping and other communications, trade, and public and private services accounted for almost 58 per cent of the Norwegian GNP; manufacturing on the other hand contributed less than 25 per cent. Even these statistics do not fully reveal the contrast with most other west European economies, for much of the manufacturing industry consists of ore processing plants which cash in on the country's abundant supplies of hydro-electric power, and fish processing factories. Neither has ever been subject to heavy tariff discrimination and therefore derive little or no benefit from the existence of EFTA. Norway's export performance in the first decade after the association was founded clearly illustrates this conclusion (Figures 17 and 18). While exports to Europe in general grew considerably, it was the EEC countries, rather than the other EFTA members, that took the greatest share of the increase.

Under such circumstances it may seem strange that Norway had anything to do with EFTA in the first place, but this is to ignore the country's strong ties, both with the rest of Scandinavia and with the United Kingdom. In 1960 these countries bought 43 per cent of Norway's exports and it would have been somewhat foolhardy to become isolated from such important markets, even if the main items of trade were not included in the EFTA agreement. Similar arguments very nearly led Norway to join the EEC in 1972, but pressure of public opinion, heavily influenced by the farming and fishing lobbies, which wanted no part of the CAP forced its application to be withdrawn at the last minute.

On the other hand, the rest of the EFTA countries benefited considerably from greater access to Norway's domestic market. Imports from these countries increased by an annual average of 11·8 per cent between 1960 and 1970 and accounted for 44·6 per cent of total imports in 1970. Although the population of 3·4 million (1970) is tiny compared with most of its European neighbours, it was still an attractive market and in many ways it was the other members who wanted to keep Norway in, rather than Norway's desire to stay.

Recently the country's capacity to exercise independence from European trade agreements has been strengthened by the discoveries of North Sea oil. Oil is raw material which will sell freely on the open market and help to disguise the limited extent of manufacturing industry. In the long-term it is possible that the imbalance could be damaging, but in the immediate future Norway seems set not merely to survive, but to flourish as a small, self-contained economic unit.

Finland

On the eastern side of the Baltic Sea, Finland had little option but to throw in its lot with EFTA, even though the move caused the government considerable political embarrassment. The country had close traditional cultural and economic links with Sweden and, in common with the rest of Scandinavia, had developed very strong trade links with the United Kingdom during the 1950s. In 1960 the United Kingdom bought nearly a quarter of Finland's exports. Nevertheless the political objections to Finnish membership of EFTA were formidable. The Finns had fought against the Soviet Union in the Second World War and, after 1945, the price they had to pay for continued independence was a strict policy of non-alliance. Even an association as politically unambitious as EFTA was felt by the government to be potentially compromising to their delicate relationship with the Soviet Union. It was only after much hesitation that they finally agreed to become associate members of the association in 1961. It was a special status that allowed Finland to continue to obtain a fixed proportion of its imports from the Soviet Union, but it was only agreed after strong pressure from the other Scandinavian countries, aware of the damage to the Finnish economy if they all had preferential treatment in the United Kingdom market. The other members were decidedly unenthusiastic about the compromise, because they felt it identified EFTA too closely with the Communist bloc. Both Austria and Switzerland believed it might prejudice their neutral status and the United Kingdom was afraid it could jeopardize a future agreement with the EEC.

In 1961 Finland's economy was similar to that of both Norway and Sweden in that it had a small number of highly productive and modern industries, which stood out from the poorly organized and generally unprofitable mass of firms. The pulp and paper industries, specialist shipbuilding and selected branches of the engineering industry had all been highly successful and were very competitive in world markets. However farming and the footwear and textile industries, all of which were important employers, were poorly equipped to cope with free competition in an open west European market. Given this structure the impact of EFTA membership was predictable: the overall volume of trade, especially with the other seven members, increased dramatically, but relatively little progress was made in diversifying the economy. Mattson, looking back over ten years of Finnish membership, spelt out the following somewhat unenthusiastic assessment: 'Looking back at the sixties and knowing the economy's structural weaknesses, it may be said that the ten years with EFTA did not wipe out the basic problems. Nor was this to be expected. One should avoid pinning false hopes in the role of customs duties for rapidly solving structural deficiencies.'[5] The major difficulty that Finland had to face was a balance of payments deficit. Other EFTA members found a ready market there for their goods, but the Finns found it harder to establish reciprocal foreign markets for their own goods. Nevertheless, even though the benefits of the free trade area were less than were hoped, they were still tangible and, when the United Kingdom and Denmark joined the EEC, Finland was as keen as all the other members to sign a trade agreement with the Community. That they were able to do so was also a tribute to the discrete political success of EFTA. By 1972 all the political reservations had disappeared; no longer were there any serious fears that Finnish membership of European organizations would give the Soviet Union a lever with which to influence the pattern of west European trade.

Denmark

No EFTA member exploited the economic potential of the free trade association more successfully than Denmark, yet originally it was the most unenthusiastic of all the members. As a country with an economy primarily dependent on agricultural exports, it seemed improbable that it would derive much benefit from free trade in industrial goods. In fact, twelve years of membership saw Denmark steadily reducing its dependence on agricultural exports to the United Kingdom and rapidly expanding its exports of manufactured goods, especially to the rest of Scandinavia. Much of the credit for this welcome diversification is now attributed to EFTA.

In the late 1950s heavy dependence on agricultural exports to Britain determined the Danish government's whole policy towards European integration. They decided to follow the United Kingdom as closely as possible in all its moves. This led them to strongly support the plan for a single all-inclusive west European free trade area in 1958, to become members of EFTA in 1960, and to make two unsuccessful applications to join the EEC in 1961 and 1967, before they were finally admitted in 1972. It was a remarkably consistent approach to foreign policy, but over the years not only had the country's economic infrastructure changed, its export markets had also broadened considerably. As a member of EFTA Denmark was free to operate its own tariff system for imports from third countries and, by keeping these as low as possible, it was able to buy industrial raw materials and semi-finished products from all over the world at the lowest possible prices. These imports formed the basis of a whole range of high technology industries, such as electronics, whose products found a ready market in the rest of Scandinavia. Denmark's trade nearly doubled between 1960 and 1970 and Norway and Sweden's share of the export market grew from 13·5 per cent to 24·1 per cent, most of the growth being in high quality manufactured goods, rather than foodstuffs. By the same token, the United Kingdom share fell from 26·6 per cent to 18·9 per cent. However it was not just the new manufacturing industries that benefited from EFTA membership, agriculture too was able to flourish. Although most of the products were excluded from the terms of the Stockholm Convention, the continuous dialogue, generated by the regular ministerial meetings in the EFTA Council helped to open up and develop new markets for agricultural products as well.

When Denmark did finally become a member of the EEC, the changes in the structure of its economy meant that it was much better prepared to withstand the competitive pressures of the Treaty of Rome. Danish farmers had always looked forward eagerly to being able to share in the high prices for farm products within the EEC, but, like the United Kingdom, Denmark had pursued a cheap food policy at home, which made the CAP unattractive to the consumers. The industrial growth and diversification that occurred throughout the 1960s largely as a result of EFTA membership, created a much higher general level of incomes, which made it easier for the Danes to accept the inevitable rise in food prices. There was also an eagerness to try and sell their newly developed manufactured goods in the European Community, a market that had been seriously neglected in the past. It could be argued of course that the new developments would have occurred with, or without EFTA, but there are good reasons for supposing that had Denmark been a member of the EEC from the first, there would not have been the same stimulus for the change of emphasis towards manufacturing industry. The high farm prices in the EEC would have tended to sustain agriculture and the common tariff would have denied Denmark access to the cheap raw materials, which gave such an important initial stimulus to industrial development.

The United Kingdom

From the very first the United Kingdom stood apart from the other members in EFTA. It was the British who first put forward the idea of a European free trade area and, with more than half the total population in the seven countries (56 million), they were bound to dominate both its initial form and subsequent development. There were, however, other reasons why Britain's role differed. More than any of the other members, it saw EFTA as a bargaining point to keep alive the concept of a larger European free trade area, for which it had fought so hard, prior to the signing of the Treaty of Rome. In this sense British motives for joining EFTA were just as much political as economic. Another important difference was the fact that three quarters of Britain's trade was not with Europe at all, so that it had many other commercial interests to nurture, most of them more lucrative than trade with its EFTA partners. Even taking European trade on its own, the United Kingdom did 25 per cent more trade with the EEC countries in 1960 than with EFTA. The final difference was in the United Kingdom's industrial structure. Already the country had a highly diversified industrial economy based on manufacturing, and what the United Kingdom government was trying to do, throughout the 1960s, was to restructure industries and redeploy resources, rather than starting from scratch.

In these circumstances it was inevitable that EFTA's contribution to the United Kingdom economy would be on a much smaller scale than elsewhere and it followed that periodically other considerations would be paramount. This was what happened in 1961, 1967 and 1971, when the United Kingdom made its three applications to join the EEC. It was also the explanation behind the introduction of the import surcharge in 1964. The United Kingdom's failure to inform its other EFTA partners of its proposed action beforehand caused considerable anger, but in fact it was less a calculated insult than a minor omission by the British. The surcharge was not primarily directed against imports from EFTA, since these were only a minor component of the United Kingdom's overall import bill.

Nevertheless the contribution of EFTA to the United Kingdom was not only to give moral support in its fight to become a member of the EEC. The United Kingdom's terms of trade were significantly altered in the 1960s and EFTA played an important role in the change. Throughout the twelve years that the United Kingdom was a member trade with its partners grew disproportionately. The distribution of exports remained much the same, despite the increased volume, but the pattern of imports exhibited a number of new features. Scandinavia had traditionally had strong commercial links with the United Kingdom and these were largely responsible for their initial membership of EFTA. Once the association began to function, however, these countries began to export relatively less to the United Kingdom and to increase their volume of trade with each other and with the other EFTA members. The United Kingdom's main export successes were with Austria, Switzerland and Portugal. In other words, one of the effects of EFTA membership for the United Kingdom was to broaden the scope of the country's trade links in Europe. Nevertheless against this success must be placed the fact that throughout the period the United Kingdom's exports to and imports from the EEC countries consistently expanded faster than those with its EFTA partners. For this reason alone there was always considerable pressure from the country's business and industrial interests for eventual membership of the European Community. There was widespread relief in 1972 when the doubts about this issue seemed to be finally resolved and the United Kingdom joined in an alliance with the other major economies of western Europe.

Portugal

Like the United Kingdom, Portugal also stood out among the EFTA countries, but for completely different reasons. In comparison with all the others it was a developing country: even in 1970 the per capita income of its 9 million inhabitants was still less than £300. Although the economy has grown rapidly with the help of EFTA membership, estimates show that it will be the end of the century before the level of development will compare with that of its partners.[6] One of the main impediments to more speedy progress is the dominant role of agriculture. In 1950, 50 per cent of the labour force was employed on the land and although the proportion had dropped to 40 per cent by 1970, agriculture still only contributes about 20 per cent to the gross national product. As a result farm workers have a very low standard of living and, unless they can be syphoned off to industrial jobs in the urban areas, they will continue to hold back Portugal's general economic development.

The special problems facing Portugal were recognized from the outset and, under the terms of the Stockholm Convention, it was allowed ten years longer than the rest of the signatories, before it would be obliged to finally remove all restrictions on free trade. At the same time the Portuguese were granted free access to other EFTA markets at the same time as the rest of the members, thus giving a considerable fillip to the country's small, but growing manufacturing sector. In addition to the weaknesses in agriculture, there were also limitations in the industrial structure, which unfortunately made it difficult for Portugal to take full advantage of the more open market. Most of the firms were small and therefore found it hard to compete with major European companies. There was also a very limited range of manufacturing industry and what there was tended to be concentrated in the labour intensive and therefore less productive sectors. For instance, textile industries were very prominent, but there was virtually no development in the electronics field, which had been the basis of industrial expansion in Denmark during the 1960s. Finally the country also had to cope with the added burden of a political dictatorship, which did not really want to see the peasant economy replaced by an urban-industrial one. Although this situation has changed since the revolution in April 1975, Portugal still lacks the political stability necessary for sustained economic growth.

The impact of EFTA on the Portuguese economy is difficult to assess, because of the long transition period and the relative underdevelopment of the economy. Nevertheless there has been both an absolute and a relative increase in trade with its partners (Figures 17 and 18), which has given a vital stimulus to the whole economy. But the main benefits are less direct. When Portugal first joined EFTA it was primarily because of its close traditional trade links with the United Kingdom. For political as well as economic reasons the country was rather isolated from the rest of western Europe. Membership of the association has gone a long way towards changing that situation, for it has drawn Portugal much more closely into the mainstream of economic discussions. Not only did the government enjoy the advantages of more frequent contact with the other EFTA governments, it also found itself in a much better position to negotiate with the EEC as one of a group of industrial nations. Had it not been a member, it is doubtful whether Portugal would have succeeded in signing a trade agreement with the Community in 1972.

Iceland

Iceland's application to join EFTA in 1968 was a tribute to the success of the organization. An extra 200,000 people made little difference to the functioning of the association, but the fact that they wanted to join the free trade area showed how far the whole process of integration had progressed in Europe in a little over ten years. In the late 1950s, small countries like Iceland and Eire did not think it worthwhile to be associated with the new international groupings; by the late 1960s they were beginning to feel distinctly isolated from the mainstream of events in Europe.

Iceland's economy, like that of Portugal, is poorly developed. The country has a much higher general standard of living, but fishing and the associated processing industries are the country's main sources of income. The lack of diversity makes it hard for Iceland to exploit fully the free trade advantages of EFTA and, for this reason, the country was granted concessions, similar to those worked out for Portugal, which mean that it will only be subject to the full force of competition from its partners after 1980.

The Success of the EFTA Experiment

Unlike the European Community, EFTA never intended to develop an identity of its own, or to be successful or unsuccessful independent of the constituent members. This being the case and given the diversity and different expectations of the signatories to the Stockholm Convention, it is hard to generalize about the association except in the various national contexts. Even so the bureaucracy of EFTA, like that of any other organization, in the end is self-perpetuating and, over the years, the Council has commissioned several studies to highlight the effectiveness of the trading group it represents. The most recent of these analyses was published in 1972 and, though only dealing with the period 1959 to 1967, it comes to some interesting conclusions.[7] The first years of EFTA's existence saw unprecedented economic growth in all the member countries, with the exception of the United Kingdom, and this created a considerable amount of new trade, most of which was kept within EFTA, rather than being spread among third party countries as well. In addition the creation of EFTA diverted existing trade in many countries towards other members of the association. All the EFTA countries shared in the new commercial activity, but Scandinavia was quite disproportionately successful. 'There is no room for doubt that the formation of EFTA has acted as a stimulus to all its members, but within the Nordic area the most rapid rise of trade has been evident.'[8] Initially EFTA was also rather more successful at stimulating trade among its members, than was the EEC with its members. To read too much into this conclusion would however be unjustified, since the wider aims of the EEC meant that it was slower than EFTA in achieving the specific aim of free trade which EFTA had as its sole concern.

Despite such reservations EFTA was much more successful at stimulating trade than any of its members dared to hope in 1960. At that time it was primarily an *ad hoc* grouping, designed to bring pressure on the European Community to create a wider European free trade area. Most analysts dismissed it rather lightly. Dell, writing in 1963, described EFTA in the following terms: 'The difference between this approach and that of the EEC again serves to emphasize the character of EFTA as a low tariff club designed to exert pressure on the EEC rather than as a serious exercise in economic integration.'[9] It achieved that goal in 1972, but by that time there were many who felt that its contribution to European economic integration was greater than that of the European Community.

7

The European Coal and Steel Community: A Pioneering Attempt at Supranational Government

The Genesis of ECSC

The High Authority of the ECSC was the first attempt at supranational government in post-war Europe. Under the terms of the Treaty of Paris, it theoretically had the powers to make and implement laws without direct recourse to the six member governments of the Community. Its creation was therefore an extremely important step in the history of political and economic integration, and its successes and failures are significant, not only for their own sake, but also for their influence on later developments.

Nevertheless, despite the lofty ideals of Jean Monnet, the first president of the ECSC, the organization was very much a product of its time and came into being as a result of the immediate, short-term economic needs of west European countries, in particular France. The object was to take the coal and steel industries, and more especially European trade in coal and steel, out of the direct control of national governments and to create a common market under the collective control of the Community. Pressure for such action was intense, because the International Ruhr Authority, set up by the Allied occupying powers in Germany in April 1949, had failed to create an adequate basis for reintegrating the German coal and steel industries into the European economy. Part of the problem was that the International Ruhr Authority was charged with trying to fulfil two conflicting objectives. On the one hand German coal was desperately required by other European countries, France in particular, and the Authority needed to increase output and to supervise the allocation between domestic consumption and exports. On the other hand there was a strong lobby in favour of holding Germany's steel output as low as possible and restricting it to peaceful uses, so as to keep the nation's military potential under a tight rein. The whole situation became untenable in the early 1950s, when there was a general shortage of steel in both North America and western Europe, and when the potential of the Ruhr conurbation was being severely limited for political reasons. The Schuman Plan for the ECSC provided an elegant way out of the impasse. International control of the Ruhr was to be effectively continued, but in a way which was permanently acceptable to the Germans, who were to be equal partners in the new Community.

The role of the French in the whole complex history of the ECSC is crucial. Initially they were the organization's most enthusiastic backers, because they believed it would guarantee steady supplies of much needed German coal to French industry on favourable terms. It was on this basis that Monnet was able to sell the idea to the French Foreign Minister, Robert Schuman, and he in turn used the same arguments to persuade the French cabinet. Without this pressure it is unlikely that the Treaty of Paris would ever have been signed. However the French became distinctly more lukewarm and even hostile towards the whole concept of supranational control of the coal and steel industries. In 1954 the French government reasserted its powers of price control in the steel industry in direct contravention of the Treaty and its refusal to co-operate on other issues severely limited the effectiveness of the High Authority. In the late 1950s the appearance of cheap US coal imports and the emergence of oil as an alternative source of energy further weakened French (and the other members') interest in the ECSC. These developments also exposed the disadvantages of limiting any supranational economic planning venture to two groups of products, however vital they might appear at a particular point in time. The most important lesson of the ECSC however was the way in which it illustrated that the strength of a supranational authority is dependent upon the consent and co-operation of member governments. Budgetary limitations and the lack of any real means of enforcing decisions make organizations like the ECSC almost entirely dependent upon their goodwill.

The Treaty of Paris itself of course did not refer to the political horse-trading which had spawned it. Its fundamental objective, set out in Article 4, was the permanent removal of all restrictions on trade in coal and steel within the member states. These included import and export duties, quota restrictions on trade, subsidies and all other conceivable forms of state assistance. In addition, price controls imposed unilaterally by member governments were to be lifted. There were all kinds of conflicting opinions as to the impact of such changes, which was hardly surprising, since prior experience of supranational government was so limited. The main elements in this spectrum of opinion have been neatly summarized by Nicholls in a study of the ECSC prepared for the American Rand Corporation:

> Coal and steel producers were afraid that their industries would be dominated by control from above, from which there would be less prospect of escape than from the control exercized by the member governments. They spoke of dirigisme and bureaucracy, and of international socialism. In turn, others saw in the High Authority a means open to the producers to re-establish the international cartels that were of such prominence in the period between the two World Wars. German industrialists, it was argued, would dominate the cartels, because of their superior productive ability.[1]

A quarter of a century later such extreme views seem somewhat naïve and unnecessarily alarmist, but they do reflect the general uncertainty surrounding the whole venture at its inception.

Achievements of the High Authority

The activities of the High Authority of the ECSC between 1952 and the merging of the European Communities in 1967 fall into three distinct areas: the removal of all barriers to free trade, including every form of government subsidy, and the creation of a system ensuring the maximum possible competition; direct management of the Community coal and steel industries; and remedial measures to assist workers and regions affected by the general run down in coal mining and, to a lesser extent, in the steel industry.

The Common Market

In the general climate of economic expansion pertaining throughout the greater part of the 1950s the High Authority found it relatively easy to persuade member governments to relax and gradually do away with many of the tariffs and quotas, which hitherto had surrounded trade in coal and iron and steel products. In fact as Diebold has pointed out, by the time the common market really began to come into effect in 1953 and 1954, there were relatively few tariffs and quotas actually in operation.[2] Outside Italy, which was a special case, the only tariff on coal, iron ore, scrap and ordinary steel being levied at the time was a small tax on ordinary steel imposed by the Benelux countries.

The outlawing of such levies had little immediate impact as a result, but it meant that any move to reimpose them in the future was strictly illegal. The ease with which the proposals could be implemented also meant that the ECSC got off to an active, but uncontroversial start. As early as 10 February 1953 all tariffs and quotas on trade in coal, iron ore and scrap were abolished. A similar agreement for ordinary steel was reached on 1 May 1953 and for alloy steels on 1 August 1954. The only major exception was a series of concessions made to the Italians, because of the special difficulties under which their relatively small-scale and isolated coal and iron and steel industries had to labour. A special annex to the Treaty allowed them a transitional period to remove duties on coal and steel, provided that these were progressively reduced and completely abolished after five years on 10 February 1958.

Against this background it is hard to accept wholeheartedly some of the more extravagant claims of the High Authority about the impact of the ECSC on the pattern of trade in coal and steel within the Community. In 1956 an analysis of the results of the first three years showed that trade in the common market had risen three times as fast as production, and that the ratio was much more favourable than for manufactured products in general.[3] It was claimed that the

Table 5 IMPORT DUTIES ON SELECTED STEEL PRODUCTS BEFORE AND AFTER THE TARIFF OF FEBRUARY 1958

	Per cent ad valorem					
	Benelux and Germany		France		Italy	
Product	before (B: Benelux; G: Germany)	after	before	after	before	after
Bars	3 B 10 G	5	10	6	22	9
Wire rods	4 B 12 G	6	12	7	13	10
Strip	6 B 15 G	8	12	9	23	10
Flat products	3–4 B 8–22 G	5–6	11–22	6	22–23	9–10
Sections	3–8 B 10–11 G	5–6	11–22	6	22–23	9–10

Source: L. Lister, *Europe's coal and steel community*, p. 344.

abolition of tariffs and quotas had led directly to the increase in production and that regional specialization in the iron and steel industries had produced a disproportionate growth in the volume of trade to the benefit of all six national economies. The facts are not in dispute, but the interpretation of the underlying cause of the trade is less than convincing. As explained above, virtually no restrictive practices were removed as a result of ECSC legislation, it simply became illegal to impose such measures in the future. The High Authority is therefore somewhat overstating its case in claiming direct credit for the upturn in trade. Success came later when, during the economic recession between 1958 and 1960, it was able to forestall any moves to reimpose tariffs and quotas. Membership of the ECSC and other similar organizations has made it much more difficult for national governments to act unilaterally to try to protect their own interests and there is no question but that this is a major step forward in managing the international economy.

The ECSC was less successful however in removing restrictive practices, other than tariffs and quotas. On the question of imports from third countries agreement was reached on most steel products by the end of the transitional period in February 1958. As can be seen in Table 5 there was a general reduction in import duties right across the board in all six countries, but a certain amount of national differentiation was retained reflecting the problems facing the steel industry in different parts of the Community.[4] The duties were lowest in the Benelux countries and Germany, where the level was on average between 5 and 6 per cent, and highest in Italy, where the level was between 9 and 10 per cent. In France the duties varied from 6 to 9 per cent. It is important to note that although import duties were reduced, nowhere were they completely abolished. On the question of coal imports there was almost no progress. Before 1958, this seemed of little consequence, since they only played a minor role in any of the member countries, but later, when there was world over-production in the 1960s, cheap American imports posed a serious threat to the mining industry throughout the ECSC, and the High Authority found itself almost powerless to deal with the situation for want of any common policy.

The most pernicious and frustrating aspect of the High Authority's long fight to remove barriers to free trade in coal and steel was transport subsidies. Manipulation of freight rates could be almost as effective as tariffs and quotas for controlling the market price of coal and steel in Europe and member governments were in a unique position to exercise such influence. Any product with low value per unit of weight inevitably incurs relatively high transport charges, if it has to be moved any distance, and most of the products of the coal and steel industries fall into this category. Indeed the increase in trade that occurred during the 1950s only served to underline the problem. The railways were the main carrier and, since they were nationalized in all the ECSC countries, governments could manipulate the rates almost at will. Nor were the effects of this limited to the railways, for at that time they held such a dominant position in the transport market as a whole, that other carriers, in particular inland waterways, were forced to compete with them for business. Obviously individual governments used their power to influence the market price of coal and steel quite consciously in some instances, but in general the overall pricing structure on the railways was so totally divorced from the economics of operating a railway network, that subsidies were often granted quite unwittingly. State control of the railways stretched back to the middle of the nineteenth century, when the networks were first built and a genuinely competitive freight rate structure had never been allowed to develop. By the time the ECSC was formed the situation almost defied logic and provoked the general manager of the French railways into commenting that: 'there are as many discriminations as there are rates.'[5] The problem was particularly acute in the coal and steel industries, for not only were a high proportion of their costs effectively transport charges, but much of their traffic was along little used specialized routes, linking isolated regions and industries to the main rail network and these were the most heavily subsidized.

The High Authority did have some success in removing the more blatant forms of discrimination, such as varying freight rates according to the origin of the shipment, and treating an international trip as though it were two national ones and thus reducing the potential for discount on the overall length of the journey. In the main though it was only able to scratch the surface of rail subsidies and had virtually no effect at all on rates charged by other carriers. For instance, the High Authority was never able to persuade the Central Rhine Commission to publish the full rate structure for shipping on the Rhine and it was therefore never in a position to even exert any influence over the railways' main competitor for coal and steel traffic in Europe.

The final major element in the High Authority's strategy to create a true common market in coal and steel was price publication. Under the terms of the Treaty of Paris all prices, both for individual products and for transport had to be published, but in the event rigid adherence to this worked against the best interests of a common market. When demand exceeded supply customers persuaded the producers to give them preferential treatment by offering prices above those published, and in the reverse situation, when there was a slump in sales, manufacturers indulged in secret price cutting. Nevertheless, a degree of uniformity was achieved in prices, even if the standard tended to be widely ignored at times, especially during periods of recession.

In the final analysis the success or failure of these individual policies were only important in relation to the broader objective of the High Authority, to create and maintain a system that ensured competition. Since the coal and steel industries were quite separately organized, despite their deep dependence upon each other, it is not surprising that the effect of the ECSC on the two industries showed marked differences. In the case of coal mining, there was a heavy government stake in the industry in all six member countries and overall 42 per cent of coal production in the Community was nationalized. This meant that any interference by the High Authority was almost automatically seen as direct intervention in an area of national policy and, however much the member governments agreed with supranational management in principle, they all found it difficult to accept when it impinged directly on their own activities. In fact the situation was made even more difficult, because the government stake in coal marketing was even higher than in production. In France all coal imports were controlled by two government agencies, the Association Technique de l'Importation Charbonnière, which was responsible for coal imports other than those for the steel industry, and a subsidiary (ORCIS), which dealt exclusively with coal imports for the steel industry. It was effectively a national monopoly and was used as an argument by private marketing cartels in other member countries to justify their continued existence, when the High Authority tried to break them up in the interests of freer competition. The most significant and powerful of these cartels was the Central Ruhr Selling Agency, which enjoyed full government backing in its efforts to resist High Authority efforts to dismember it. The German government argued that the French ATIC was a monopoly and centralized marketing of Ruhr coal was therefore essential: the French put the opposite case. It was a classic confrontation and one which the High Authority, even through the good offices of the Court of Justice did not have the power to break.

The steel industry proved to be much more amenable to supranational control. In the first place the industry was not nationalized, except for 50 per cent of the Italian and 10 per cent of the German capacity. There was also no compulsion to sell through any centralized marketing agency. Individual producers bargained directly with the steel consumers. Finally transport costs are a smaller element in steel production than in coal production. For all these reasons, together with the fact that European steel operations are traditionally on a smaller scale than those in North America, where US Steel and the Bethlehem Steel Corporation have effectively carved up the domestic market between them, the High Authority found itself able to manage competition much more effectively than in the coal industry. Not that it was by any means totally successful. In both France and West Germany there was ample evidence of direct government intervention to influence steel prices. This was either achieved illegally in open defiance of the High Authority, or by the more circuitous route of fixing the price of goods in which steel was an important element and thereby controlling the price. This practice was not subject to the rules of the Treaty of Paris and therefore technically legal, even though it defeated the whole purpose of the ECSC.

Despite all the difficulties, the High Authority did succeed in removing many restrictive practices and barriers to freer trade in coal and steel products, although it is perhaps a moot point to what extent the relaxation of restrictions and the liberalization of trade would have occurred with or without a supranational organization like the ECSC. Certainly it is true that the activities of the High Authority made both government and private industry more aware of their restrictive practices and subsidies and they were therefore more able to control or remove them, if they so desired.

Management

The High Authority proved relatively ineffectual when it came to realizing management objectives, other than the creation of a common market. It was continually inhibited by its very limited direct access to funds and by lack of agreement among the member states, who retained a tight rein on the finances and on the form and general direction of management policies. The financial contribution of the Community to development policy has been described as 'only a drop in the bucket' and inevitably this has meant that its capacity to influence development policy has been severely limited.[6] Capital expenditure was consistently over-estimated in the coal and iron mining industries between 1954 and 1974 and, in both cases, there has been a sharp downward trend in the overall level of capital investment (Figure 19). Even in the iron and steel industry, where investment targets were more often met and where production has generally been sharply increased, there is no evidence that the ECSC was able to manage the market so as to compensate for the natural cyclic

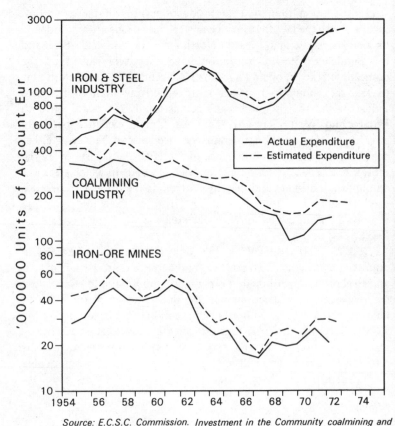

Source: E.C.S.C. Commission. Investment in the Community coalmining and iron and steel industries, July 1974

Figure 19   Actual and estimated investment in the iron and steel, coal mining and iron ore mining industries in the ECSC

demand for iron and steel. Neither has the Community been particularly successful at reallocating investment. Warren has shown that despite the fact that European coal is not suitable for coking, investment in the iron and steel industries still tends to concentrate on plant at the traditional sites on the coal and ore fields, rather than at more flexible coastal sites.[7]

The High Authority's ineffectiveness was shown up starkly by its eventual failure to produce a workable common policy for the use of scrap in the steel industry, despite the fact that all six member governments wanted it to do so. The main problem was that any ECSC policy had to incorporate the elements of the individual national policies; it was never allowed to stand in its own right and the result was a hybrid, full of contradictions. On the one hand there was a general move to discourage the use of scrap, because it was felt that the sources of supply were much less dependable than those for iron ore. On the other hand great emphasis was laid on keeping the cost of raw materials, scrap included, as low as possible, so as to ensure cheap steel supplies. In combination these two objectives made it virtually impossible to use the price mechanism to discourage the use of scrap in the steel industry. What happened in practice was that domestic scrap prices were kept artificially low and therefore relatively small amounts were produced. However, the shortage of raw materials in the mid-1950s was such, that there was a considerable increase in the volume of expensive imported scrap and this in turn eventually drove the basic price of steel upwards. This of course invalidated the whole purpose of the policy and by 1958 the High Authority itself was advocating that the working of the scrap market should be left to free market forces, without any recourse to government intervention, be it national or supranational.

The High Authority also proved ineffective in preventing the decline of the coal industry, once other sources of energy and foreign imports became more freely and cheaply available after 1958. United States coal was sold in France, the Benelux countries and Germany, and the Treaty of Paris gave the ECSC no jurisdiction over the increasing use of oil as a source of energy for industry. There was a general demand by government for a shift in policy to protect the Community coal industry from these two new sources of competition, but the members were unable to agree on the form of such protection. This resulted in 'the individual government rather than the Community being the effective unit of control, much to the disillusionment of certain observers'.[8] The French were able to control coal imports fairly easily through the Association Technique de l'Importation Charbonnière and, in addition, they imposed a tax on fuel oil to keep the price on a par with domestic coal. The Belgians and the Germans licensed coal imports from third countries and also imposed taxes on oil imports. Only the Netherlands and Italy rejected controls completely and in Italy's case, this was only because it virtually had no domestic coal industry to protect. The Community's failure to even play a co-ordinating role in the rapid policy changes of member countries in the face of the new threats was a serious setback, underlining its lack of real power. It undermined confidence in the organization and consigned it very much to the shadow of the newly formed European Economic Community after 1958.

Remedial measures

The changed economic situation in the Community after 1958 was reflected in both the coal and steel industries: over-production plagued mining and an increasing number of pits were abandoned and closed; technological improvements in the steel-making process meant that many traditional plants in Europe became uneconomic. The changes placed new demands on the ECSC; no longer was it managing the market for vital industrial raw materials, for which there was an almost insatiable demand, it now had to provide for a phased contraction of the coal industry and a radical restructuring of the steel industry. Its response was on two fronts, readaptation and reconversion. Readaptation involved retraining and redeploying workers made redundant by the contraction of the two industries; reconversion was the name given to a whole series of measures aimed at encouraging new industries to move to the older, declining industrial areas.

In the first years after the decline set in, readaptation posed few problems for the High Authority. Most of the displaced coal and steel workers found new jobs quickly in the same locality and often in the same industry. Only in the small remote industrial areas, like the Borinage in Belgium and the Auvergne and Aquitaine in France, was there any real problem and this was relatively small scale. Throughout the 1960s though, redundant workers began to find it increasingly difficult to find new jobs. There were a number of reasons for the change, including the increasing rate of decline in the overall size of the labour force, the fact that in the long-term the decline of any industry and especially heavy industry produces an overall rundown in the regional economy, and the gathering economic depression of the late 1960s and 1970s. It became quite clear that something more than the readaptation measures were required. Consequently the High Authority began to plan its reconversion policy and one of the first positive actions was to commission a detailed study of the economic and social structure of all the coal mining and steel making areas in the Community in 1962. The reports were published in 1968 and formed the basis of ECSC and later European Community reconversion policy.[9]

In practice however the readaptation and reconversion policies evolved in parallel, rather than in concert until after the merging of the three Communities in 1967. As far as readaptation was concerned the High Authority concluded separate agreements with each of the member governments on the precise form that aid should take.

Agreements were signed with West Germany, France and Belgium in 1960, Italy in 1965 and Luxembourg and the Netherlands in 1966. Although each differed in detail, they all had the same basic objectives, neatly summarized into four categories by Vinck: assistance to encourage acceptance of employment which is less well paid than the former job; assistance to facilitate re-employment in another occupation; assistance to facilitate re-employment in another region; and assistance to employees who are waiting for a new job.[10]

Readaptation assistance was open to every coal and steel concern in all the member countries on an equal basis, but there were considerable differences in the way in which it was applied, both in the two industries and in the various regions of the Community. In general the needs of coal mining were much greater than those of the steel industry, since the industry was being reduced in size rather than reorganized. West Germany, which had by far the largest mining industry, consumed nearly half of the available funds, but in proportional terms the shares of both Belgium and France were much greater. The reason for this discrepancy was that alternative sources of employment were readily available in the Ruhr, West Germany's main mining region, whereas in both France and Belgium the coal mining areas were heavily dependent upon the one industry. This was particularly true in Belgium, where mining was concentrated into two basins, the Borinage and the Centre, neither of which had any other important industrial investment. As a result, large sums had to be spent both on occupational training and on disturbance allowances. The overall contribution made by the High Authority to ease the worst effects of the run-down of coal mining in the Community was important, but should not be over-stated. The global amount of money committed was only £30 million, a fraction of the total sum used to subsidize heavy industry over the same period by national governments.

The same reservations apply even more strongly to reconversion. The High Authority has so far been involved in about fifty separate projects aimed at introducing new industrial concerns into areas afflicted by the contraction of the coal mining industry, notably in the Limburg, Liège, Centre and Borinage areas of Belgium and in the Nord/Pas de Calais and Lorraine areas of France. However, it is severely constrained by the lack of formal agreements with individual member governments such as those concluded on readaptation. In reconversion matters the High Authority can only contribute if specifically invited by a member government. It is also limited by the Treaty of Paris as to the form and extent of its initiatives, and lack of funds often further restricts the scope of such initiatives. Nevertheless the contribution of the High Authority to restructuring the Community's industrial environment has been important, for it has provided a forum for discussing mutual problems and encouraged the member governments to adopt a common approach. Finally, even though the financial contribution is small, the fact that it exists at all has meant that the High Authority has been able to exert some influence on the way in which development programmes have been planned and implemented.

The failure to develop common policies

The ECSC was a pioneering attempt at supranational government and, with the benefit of hindsight, it is obvious that the chances of it playing a permanent role in the economic fabric of an integrated Europe were dim. By limiting the scope of the organization to coal and steel, it is now clear that the whole structure was too inflexible to allow for future change. With such a limited brief it could not develop on its own initiative any major common policies for the Community economy. Industrial, transport and energy policies were all partially within its field of interest, but none wholly so. It is certainly no accident that when the Treaty of Rome was being drafted to establish the EEC, the result was much broader and not limited to specific industries. Nevertheless the failure to develop common policies was not by any means solely attributable to the specific terms of reference of the Treaty of Paris. Since the executives of the three Communities were merged in 1967, little or no further progress has been made. The fate of the Common Transport Policy is discussed in Chapter 8; the Common Industrial Policy is almost totally moribund; and the all-important Common Energy Policy is lost in a welter of words and a commitment to nuclear energy, which seems somewhat peripheral to a European economy on the verge of developing some of the world's most important oil and gas fields. The ECSC unearthed the problems of supranational government, but neither it nor the other European Communities, has merged so far to provide a convincing formula for long-term success.

8

Common Policies in the European Economic Community

The Place of Common Policies

Free enterprise and the principles of the market economy are at the very heart of the EEC, but from the outset it was widely appreciated, both by outside commentators and by those concerned with drawing up the Treaty of Rome, that certain aspects of the economic infrastructure simply could not be accommodated within such a framework. It followed that the economic union would only be achieved among the member states when there was not only free movement of products and factors of production but also harmonization of national policies, so that discrimination created by the working of these policies could be eliminated. There are therefore two distinct aspects to the whole process, which will eventually lead to union: negative integration and positive integration. Pinder defines the former as the removal of discrimination and the latter as 'the formation and application of co-ordinated common policies in order to fulfil economic and welfare objectives other than the removal of discrimination'.[1]

The distinction is clearly recognized in the Treaty of Rome, for the creation of common policies for agriculture and transport are defined as two of the basic tasks of the EEC. Both are areas where the state has played a decisive role, through a combination of ownership, financial subsidy and other forms of support, in virtually every European country. It was inconceivable that these policies of intervention should simply be abandoned after 1958. At the same time, anarchy would also have occurred if each member state had continued to pursue its own national policies unchecked. Agricultural products and transport are fundamental components in the market

145

price of most goods and differential prices and charges in these sectors would lead to distortions throughout the economy and undermine the whole concept of free competition.

In the Treaty of Rome the form of both common agricultural and transport policies are developed at some length, and there are strong guidelines about the timetable to be followed for introducing them. Agriculture is considered under Title II (Articles 38–47) and the precise objectives of the mandatory common policy are set out in Article 39:

(a) to increase agricultural productivity by promoting technical progress and by ensuring the rational development of agricultural production and the optimum utilization of the factors of production, in particular labour;

(b) thus to ensure a fair standard of living for the agricultural community, in particular by increasing the individual earnings of persons engaged in agriculture;

(c) to stabilize markets;

(d) to assure the availability of supplies;

(e) to ensure that supplies reach consumers at reasonable prices. [2]

Basically the aim was to create regular and assured supplies of food at prices the consumer would be prepared to afford and to produce stability and prosperity for the farmers. Today it is widely agreed that the two goals are mutually incompatible and that the conflict between them threatens the whole fabric of agriculture in the EEC,[3] but in 1958 there were few such doubts and the Treaty of Rome set out in some detail the mechanisms for achieving the new policy. By any standards it was a bold attack on a potentially insuperable barrier to true integration. In fact the common agricultural policy was actually expressed in such specific terms as a result of strong pressure from France and Italy, reflecting those countries' determination to secure as favourable a deal for their farming interests as West Germany was getting for its manufacturing industry. One of the major initial attractions of joining the EEC to West Germany was the prospect of free trade in industrial goods and in particular easier entry into the French market. For the French, with their larger-scale and in part more efficient agricultural industry, freer access to the 60 million consumers in West Germany was the main condition of acceptance of the general free trade principles of the Treaty.

The element of political horse-trading surrounding the early negotiations about agriculture in the EEC has been both a strength and a weakness. From the outset there has been a general sense of urgency and a determination to devise and implement an acceptable policy as quickly as possible. Throughout the 1960s the Common Agricultural Policy was by far the most important aspect of positive integration embraced by the EEC. The difficulties surrounding its establishment led the Community to the brink of disintegration on several occasions, but for all that it quickly assumed a central importance. The policy now exists, and despite its many shortcomings, it is a major cohesive element binding the members inextricably together. Each has gone a long way towards abandoning its own individual approach to agricultural subsidy and support, so that a single EEC policy may be created and, for this reason alone, not one of the members is now in a position to consider withdrawal from the Common Agricultural Policy or the Community.

The history and present state of the common transport policy is quite different. No country stood to gain directly from the establishment of such a policy and, as a result, there has been a conspicuous lack of urgency both among the EEC Commission in Brussels and among the politicians of the member nations. Nevertheless, under Title IV (Articles 74–84) of the Treaty of Rome, it is mandatory that the EEC should formulate and inaugurate a common policy covering road, rail and inland waterways. The Council of Ministers, on the advice of the Commission and after having consulted both the Economic and Social Committee and the European Parliament, is duty bound to formulate the following:

(a) common rules applicable to international transport to or from the territory of a Member State or passing across the territory of one or more Member States;
(b) the conditions under which non-resident carriers may operate transport services within a Member State;
(c) any other appropriate provisions.[4]

So far the policy, such as it is, has fallen down on two grounds. First, although there has been some progress towards standardizing operating procedures, in particular for road transport, virtually nothing has been done to eliminate or standardize national subsidies for the different forms of transport. Thus basic inequalities remain and, more importantly, there is nothing approaching an EEC development and investment policy for transport. Secondly, the terms of the proposed policy, as laid down in the Treaty, are incomplete, in so far as they exclude air and sea transport and pipelines. Air and sea transport were already subject to international agreements in the 1950s and, partly in deference to these arrangements, they were not included directly, although provision was made under Article 84 for them to be covered by a common transport policy in the future. In any case neither played a very important role in the internal movement of either goods or persons within the EEC at the time the Treaty was signed. Since then air transport has greatly expanded and its role has been further enhanced by the accession of Denmark, Eire and the United Kingdom, so that there are much stronger arguments for including it in any discussions. Pipelines illustrate the difficulty of coping with a new technology. In 1958 their role was insignificant. Now not only are they the main means of transporting oil, the most important single source of energy in the EEC, their use is also being extended to other bulk products. Pipelines are already having an impact on other forms of freight transport, in that traffic is being diverted from traditional carriers, in particular the inland waterways and the railways. Since it is some of the most lucrative traffic that is being syphoned away, the transfer is a serious threat to the overall viability of these more ubiquitous forms of freight transport.

This latter point serves to underline one of the fundamental criticisms of the common policies for positive integration pursued so far by the EEC; that they are too disjointed and limited in scope. So far the tendency has been to take specific problems and to look at them in isolation, rather than attempting to develop an integrated approach involving all sections of the economy. It was this doubt, together with the realization that there was little provision in the Treaty of Rome for helping depressed industrial regions, that led the United Kingdom to press for the setting up of an EEC Regional Policy as a precondition of its joining the Community. A Regional Development Fund was agreed in principle in 1972 and the details of a three-year programme announced in 1973. At present the emphasis is heavily biased towards peripheral industrial development, but in the future it seems only logical that the Fund will have to co-ordinate all aspects of structural reform, be they in the fields of industry, agriculture or transport.

The Common Agricultural Policy (CAP)

Although the need for a common agricultural policy was accepted from the outset by the six original members of the EEC, its precise form and overall significance in the future structure of the Community were far less clear and more open to argument. To appreciate fully the complexity of the issues involved the background to the industry in each of the member countries must be clearly understood. Only then is it possible to see why the CAP developed as it did and why it has failed to achieve some of its objectives as laid down in the Treaty of Rome.

The Background to the Industry

In 1958 agriculture was one of the main elements in the economy of every west European country; in the six prospective members of the EEC the industry employed 17½ million people, about 20 per cent of the working population. The heavy concentration was primarily due to a complex series of national protection policies, which had shielded European farmers from the generally more competitive world markets. In common with virtually all other industrialized countries, agriculture in Europe had moved out of the realm of economic competition proper and had degenerated into what may loosely be called a competition for subsidies, with each country trying to shift its agricultural difficulties onto others by mutually offsetting protective measures.[5] The net result was an inordinately large number of people in agricultural employment and an industry that had failed to adapt to technological and economic change. In West Germany, Italy and to a lesser extent in France mechanization had proceeded only slowly: small farm units made it difficult to finance and justify large-scale capital investment, and many farms were in any case extremely marginal and only able to survive at all by virtue of subsidies and other forms of support.

Throughout the Community there was a general commitment to direct government intervention in the working of the industry, but there were important differences in the approach adopted by the member countries. The Netherlands had traditionally pursued an aggressive and expansionist policy, with a view to developing agriculture as a major part of its overall export economy. The industry was well organized and production and marketing were geared towards supplying foreign markets. In Belgium and Germany on the other hand the national policies were essentially defensive and unashamedly protectionist. Consumers were expected to pay high prices for food in order to keep the domestic industry alive, but little thought was given by government towards promoting agricultural exports and thereby offsetting some of the costs of the system of domestic subsidies. In France and Italy the traditional policies were very similar to those in Belgium and Germany, but both these countries saw in the EEC an opportunity to revitalize their flagging domestic industries. Each had considerable underutilized agricultural capacity in the form of rural land which could either be brought into production or used more intensively, and the promise of higher prices elsewhere in the Community, particularly in West Germany, made the prospect of agricultural expansion an appealing one. In this respect the example of the Netherlands was an object lesson in what could be achieved by careful planning and organization.

In addition to these fundamental differences in the way in which the industry was organized, there were also other more practical difficulties to be overcome. Each country had its own particular problems and interests, and naturally they were all determined to ensure that these were accommodated in the CAP. In France and Italy, for example, productivity, both in terms of yields per hectare and in output per animal were less than half what they were in the Netherlands, a reflection of the underutilized capacity referred to above. A major concern of both these countries therefore was to ensure that the CAP stimulated output, even though food production in the EEC as a whole was more than sufficient already and any increases were likely to produce surpluses. To sell any such excess on the world market would be difficult, since production costs and food prices in Europe were generally above world levels. Another crucial obstacle was structural reform. The infrastructure of the agricultural industry in all the EEC countries was poor, but the precise nature of the problems varied considerably and it was hard to devise a single strategy to cope with them all. In Italy and, to a lesser extent in Germany and Belgium, the average size of holdings was too small and a reduction in the number of farms through a programme of phased amalgamation was essential in order to make the industry as a whole viable. The most urgent problem in Germany however was land consolidation. Mayhew has estimated that some 8·69 million hectares required consolidation in 1968 and even the projected cost was DM 1245 million.[6] For its part France was less interested in structural reform than in high prices for farm produce and, as a result, there was disagreement as to whether the CAP should put most of its effort into guaranteed prices or structural reform. There was also argument about the allocation of priorities among the various types of structural reform. The final major area of difficulty was in accommodating the various patterns of agricultural production in the different EEC countries within the confines of a single policy. In Italy more than 60 per cent of the farm produce was in the form of labour intensive crops like fruit and vegetables, whereas in France and Germany the proportions were roughly 40 per cent and 30 per cent respectively. Naturally therefore a support system favouring direct subventions to the workforce would be more acceptable to the Italian authorities than one which subsidized capital investment and equipment. The converse was the case in Germany and the Netherlands, where there was a greater concentration on the more capital intensive livestock production and a consequently greater desire to see help for capital investment programmes and subsidies for raw materials, in particular animal feedstuffs. It is not simply that livestock farming is more capital intensive than market gardening and arable farming generally, but incomes for livestock farmers are much more sensitive to price fluctuations beyond their control, because of the dependence on outside sources of supply for foodstuffs and plant.

Despite the general agreement on the need for a common agricultural policy, not every member brought the same sense of urgency to the difficult task of reaching agreement. In Germany and Luxembourg agriculture's share of the Gross Domestic Product was under 5 per cent, but in France and the Netherlands it was over 7 per cent and in Italy nearly 12 per cent. These differences were obviously reflected in the enthusiasm with which the negotiations about a common policy were pursued. Each national negotiator was also subject to domestic pressure from regional groups in his home country. The broad generalizations about the structure of agriculture in each of the member countries hide important regional variations and inequalities. This is particularly true of France where the large-scale agriculture in the Paris Basin and the eastern half of the country disguises a poorly organized and uncoordinated industry in the west and south. Structural reform was urgently required in areas like Brittany and farmers from this, and other regions, were determined to ensure that their interests did not suffer within the wider framework of the EEC. Minority groups such as the Bretons quickly found that they could exert considerable influence on the negotiations in Brussels and they were not slow to use it. Similar discrepancies were to be found in most of the other countries and, as a result, there was virtually no room for real concessions by any of the parties and, as negotiations progressed, there came to be some justification in the jibe that the CAP was no more than the sum of the protective practices of the six member countries, rather than a new policy resulting from a process of give and take.

The Birth of a Common Policy

Against this background of long-standing government intervention in agriculture and its finances, the European Commission moved rapidly to initiate discussions about a common policy immediately the Treaty of Rome had been signed. In July 1958 a meeting was convened in Stresa at which guidelines for the future of European agriculture were worked out by delegates representing both governments and the industry. Although inevitably only general principles were discussed,

two important points did emerge. There was general agreement
that the family structure of farming should as far as possible be
preserved. This was an important decision, because in effect it was a
commitment not to allow economic and technological pressures to
destroy the pre-industrial social structure of the industry. It also followed that the cost of producing agricultural products in Europe was
likely to remain high in the foreseeable future, since the family farm
was far from the ideal economic unit. The meeting also agreed to
accept the generalized provisional timetable, set out rather vaguely
in the Treaty of Rome. Three basic stages were proposed: an initial
three-year period when the general outline of the policy would be
discussed and agreed; a gradual integration and alignment of existing
national policies into the new CAP, which was to be completed not
later than the beginning of 1970; and a final stage when outstanding
anomalies would be ironed out. These conclusions were quickly
accepted by the Council of Ministers, so that work on developing a
common policy for the whole of the community was able to start
almost as soon as the Treaty came into force.

Given the basic interventionist stance of all the member governments there was in fact relatively little room for manoeuvre when it
came to actually drawing up a common policy for agriculture.[7] The
only really practical approach was for each state to gradually dismantle its own protection policy and to substitute a common EEC
system. Other possible solutions ruled themselves out in practice, not
least on political grounds. On the face of it, for example, there were
strong arguments for excluding agricultural products from the common market, because of the difficulty of assimilating them into a free
trade system, but, as has already been explained, France and Italy
regarded free access for their agricultural products to a wider European market as one of the main benefits they stood to gain from
joining the EEC. Another possible option was to abandon subsidies
altogether for a common external tariff on agricultural imports, but
this was equally unrealistic because of the social and economic dis-
ruption it would inevitably have caused in many parts of the Community. One of the main purposes of all the support measures was to
reduce the growing discrepancies between rural and urban incomes,
and any serious move to abolish subsidies would have had the opposite
effect and created considerable unrest in marginal areas like Schleswig-
Holstein, Brittany and Southern Italy.

The basic objectives of the CAP, set out in general terms in the
Treaty of Rome, were stable and regular supplies of food for all and
a guaranteed livelihood for the farming community. However because

of the potential conflict between these two ideals, referred to earlier, it was necessary to re-examine and clarify the initial terms of reference. The need to maintain assured and steady supplies of all major products was absolute; there was general agreement that a high level of agricultural self-sufficiency was desirable in the EEC. It was also accepted that the balance between supply (farm output) and demand (retail consumption) would be partially managed. Increases in productivity would be offset by a reduction in the number of farms and farm workers. With a well-fed and largely static European population, there was little likelihood of significant changes in the level of retail consumption. Any growth in real incomes was unlikely to be spent on higher per capita consumption of food. It was generally agreed therefore that a smaller agricultural labour force must be the long-term objective. Not surprisingly, it was much harder to achieve a consensus on the precise mechanisms for achieving these management objectives, and there was also widespread disagreement about price levels. A compromise had to be reached which would create farm incomes high enough to cover not only production costs but also partial self-financing of investments on the larger and more efficient farms. However prices could not be set too high, otherwise they would not act as an incentive to the small and inefficient farmer to leave the land, a major objective of any policy, particularly in areas where the natural conditions did not favour agriculture. To reach agreement on such a delicate balance was virtually impossible, especially since the terms 'efficient' and 'inefficient' were as good as meaningless in such a heavily subsidized industry.

The members of the EEC quickly agreed in principle that the CAP should operate through a system of support for market prices. Price levels for individual products were to be determined centrally in Brussels as part of an annual review; cheap imports were to be excluded by variable levies, bringing the cost of non-EEC produce up to the Community price levels; and any domestic over-production was to be neutralized by central buying of surpluses by the EEC Commission through the Agriculture Fund. Where possible these surpluses would then be stored and disposed of at a later date, either at a time of shortage in the EEC itself or on the world market. In a slightly different form there was a time-honoured precedent for such a practice in the agricultural policies of the United States in the 1950s, when quotas were set for some crops, farmers were paid to keep land fallow and vast quantities of grain were stored in government silos.

The practical difficulties involved in such a radical reorganization and rationalization of national policies were enormous and the whole proposal very nearly foundered in the early years. The key to the policy was cereal prices. Grain was the basis of most animal feedstuffs and fundamental to livestock production; there could be no question of removing restrictions on trade in animal products while there were different national prices for the single most important element of production costs. Little practical progress was made until 1962, but then, under pressure from the French, the Council of Ministers decided on a programme to align not only cereal prices, but also those for pig meat, eggs, poultry meat, fruit and vegetables and wine. It was agreed that a single common price level should be in operation by the end of 1969 and in the intervening period there should be upper and lower limits for Community prices, and that this band should be progressively narrowed during the transition period. There followed a gap of nearly two years before similar arrangements were made for beef and veal, dairy products and vegetable oils and fats.

By mid-1964 it was clear that the rate of progress was too slow and the timetable to which the EEC was working too long-drawn out, so it was decided to take more immediate action on the crucial question of cereal prices. Under a revised agreement uniform price levels were to be introduced on 1 July 1967 and were to be accompanied by the abolition of levies between member countries, on cereals, pig meat, eggs and poultry. The scheme meant an inevitable drop in prices for farmers in Germany, Italy and Luxembourg, but they were to be compensated from central EEC funds on a sliding scale basis up to 1970. In 1965 however there was a major hiatus in the Community over financial control. It revolved around much wider budgetary issues than merely the CAP, although agricultural finance was inevitably an important element in the dispute. The French threatened to withdraw completely from the EEC and the matter was only settled after more than a year of argument. Despite these alarms the common cereal prices did nevertheless come into force as planned, and free movement of grain and livestock products was a fact from the beginning of July 1967 onwards. Earlier, in 1966, the Commission had put forward similar proposals for milk and milk products, beef and veal, rice, sugar, oilseeds and olive oil, and these too were accepted and came into force in 1968. The CAP was an operational reality and more than eighteen months ahead of the schedule laid down in the Treaty of Rome; the only important products not covered by it were mutton and lamb, potatoes and wood.

There remained of course the difficult problem of fixing prices at an appropriate level. There were considerable differences in price levels among the six countries, particularly where the all-important cereals were concerned. There was enormous pressure from agricultural interests on all sides to fix prices at the upper end of the scale, with the result that the standard tended to be that prevailing in the high-cost production areas, such as West Germany and Italy, thus creating considerably enhanced profits for farmers in France and the Netherlands.[8] Despite the fact that these prices are reassessed annually and notwithstanding widespread criticism from outside the EEC, the high levels have been maintained, creating something of an anomaly. Community food prices were considerably higher than in other western industrial nations in the late 1960s and early 1970s, although the increase in world commodity prices since 1973 has now largely eroded the differential.

The general concept and structure of the CAP is quite straightforward, but its day-to-day operation is complex and is often made even more difficult to understand by the specialist vocabulary used to describe the policy and its workings. The procedures vary depending on the individual product, a slightly different mechanism having been developed for each one. As an example however, the system for determining the vital cereal prices is described below.

All cereal prices in the EEC are ultimately controlled by the *target price*, which is agreed annually by the Council of Ministers in Brussels, and fixed at the level which it is assumed grain would fetch in the area of shortest supply in the EEC as a whole. Notionally this point has been defined as the city of Duisburg at the western end of the Ruhr conurbation. The target price is quoted in *units of account* and includes not only the cost of production, but also delivery, storage and other marketing costs. It also varies throughout the year between August and July, rising to take account of the increased storage costs as the farm year progresses. As long as market prices do not fall below the target price there is no interference in the process of free bargaining, but should overproduction occur within the Community and prices become depressed the EEC Commission intervenes and begins support buying. The price at which support buying begins is called the *intervention price* and is set at a predetermined percentage below the target price. The precise level is readjusted each year at the same time as the annual price review, but has usually been 7 to 8 per cent lower. There are a whole series of intervention buying centres at different locations in the EEC and the price at each varies slightly, reflecting differences in transport costs from the points of supply. The second element of the pricing system is the mechanism for dealing with imports and exports. The *threshold price* is the minimum price at which imports may be bought at EEC ports and it is calculated so that, after transport costs from the port of entry to Duisburg have been added, the grain sells in the Community at, or rather above the target price. The threshold price therefore consists of two elements: the original selling price of the grain and a *levy* to make it up to the same level as the target price. Since world prices vary the levy is re-calculated each day on the basis of the cheapest consignment of grain entering the EEC on that particular date. As most imports are more expensive than this, the system in effect ensures that grain imported into the EEC is considerably dearer than the domestic product. In the 1960s the high price of Community cereals meant that it was impossible to sell them competitively on world markets and a system of *export refunds* had to be worked out as part of the CAP. It enabled farmers who wished to sell outside the Community to quote competitive prices, secure in the knowledge that losses would be covered. Since 1973 however the position has been reversed: the recent explosion in world grain prices has made EEC cereals relatively cheap and, in order to prevent wholesale exporting, a tax has been imposed on wheat exports to discourage sales outside the Community (Figure 20).

When the CAP was conceived it was envisaged that it would have two distinct roles guaranteeing prices as described above and providing direct financial encouragement for structural reform. In practice the cost of the guarantees has been so high that very little has been done to modernize the industry. Initially it was intended that the guidance section of the budget should be set at one-third that of the guarantee section, but since 1966–7 a ceiling of 285 million units of account has been set on these activities. It is a trifling sum compared with the 2,529 million units of account spent on guarantees in the most expensive year 1969–70 and, over the Community as a whole, has had a relatively small impact on the process of structural reform. Indeed it has created a situation whereby the marketing of agricultural produce is now centrally organized, but structural reform is still a matter for national governments. For example, the West German government alone spent the equivalent of 250 million units of account on structural reform in 1974.

The financial implications of the CAP are of course enormous and constitute by far the largest single item in the EEC budget, accounting for more than 90 per cent of total expenditure. The expenses are met from the European Agricultural Guidance and Guarantee Fund (FEOGA), and in the early 1960s it was hoped that the whole policy would be virtually self-financing, with the proceeds of the import levies covering the costs of price support and structural reform. Unfortunately the huge increase in food production which the higher

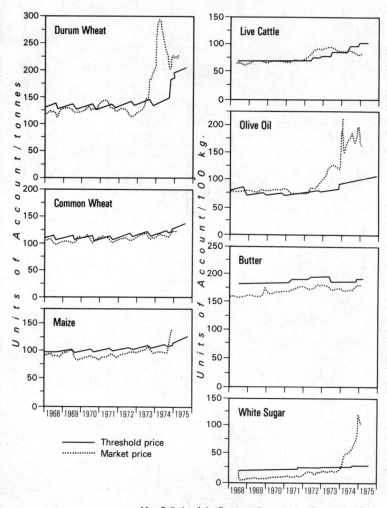

After Bulletin of the European Communities, Supplement 2/75

Figure 20   Threshold prices and market prices for selected agricultural products in the European Community

CAP prices created in the EEC meant that the Community soon became virtually self-sufficient in foodstuffs. Consequently the income from levies fell dramatically and the cost of intervention buying rose sharply, with the result that the CAP became a considerable financial liability (Figure 21). Each member country had to find large sums from its own national budget to keep the scheme afloat, and inevitably an element of disillusionment and recrimination crept into the annual negotiations. But despite the doubts and disappointments the creation

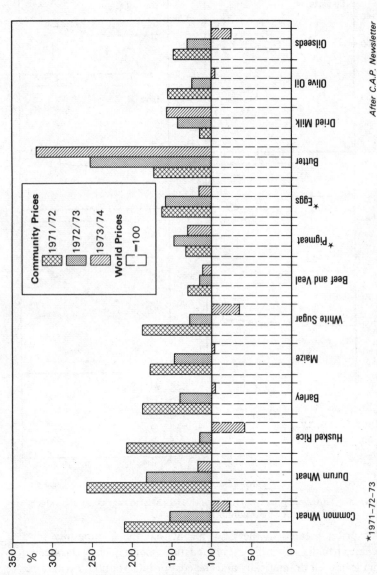

*1971–72–73

Figure 21   The relationship between world prices and Community farm prices 1971–74

After C.A.P. Newsletter

of the CAP was a unique achievement. Swann put it in its proper perspective when he said that: 'It should perhaps be noted that although the common policy is protectionist and does not make sense economically its creation was a remarkable administrative (and political) achievement. This is all the more true when it is recognized that the system covers about 90 per cent of farm output and the produce of more than 10 million operatives.'[9] National systems of price support within the Community had been virtually abolished and replaced by a single EEC system operated centrally from Brussels, and the maze of protection which formerly existed between member states had been swept away in favour of a free market.

Practical Deficiencies in the CAP

The scale of the reorganization needed to bring the CAP into being was of such magnitude that if much time had been spent by the six member governments in dwelling on the potential pitfalls and dangers the policy would never have been agreed. Even so a determination to succeed no matter what the odds did not simply remove all the problems, for it was virtually impossible to formulate any contingency plans in advance in view of so many conflicting opinions as to what would happen once the CAP was actually working. Each problem had to be dealt with on its merits as it arose. Some, such as overproduction and surpluses and the unfair distribution of contributions to the Agricultural Fund in relation to benefits received, were apparent from the outset and have already been referred to briefly, but others have only emerged as the CAP developed.

Surpluses have always been a fundamental problem and intrinsic in the CAP. Once the basic decision had been taken to encourage a high level of agricultural self-sufficiency within the Community as a whole, the latent potential for production made surpluses of some crops virtually inevitable, at least in the short-term. The only solution was either a system which matched internal supply and demand fairly precisely, or the possibility of selling any excess produce on world markets. Neither option was very practical, especially in the early years. The general upward movement of farm prices which followed the setting-up of the CAP enhanced output, but also drove EEC prices well above world levels, which meant that exports had to be subsidized from Community funds. The result was an accumulation of large surpluses of butter, beef, wheat, sugar, milk powder and most recently wine in central EEC stores, much of which had to be disposed of at a considerable economic loss. In 1973 a large quantity of butter was sold to the Soviet Union at the equivalent of 8 pence per pound, about 25 per cent of the price within the Community. Such sales were very unpopular with other agricultural trading nations. They felt they were being made the victims of unfair competition through dumping, and alternative ways of disposal had to be sought. One of the main solutions was *denaturing*, a process by which produce was made unfit for human consumption and then used as animal feedstuff. In the late 1960s large quantities of grain were disposed of in this way and in 1976 1 million tonnes of excess milk powder was similarly used up. Nonetheless it is an unhappy solution: in the first eight months of 1975 for example the EEC Commission estimated that denaturing milk powder cost the European taxpayer £339 million, an unfortunate waste of resources.

Since 1972–3 the problem of surpluses has been dramatically reduced as the result of a general rise in world food prices (Figure 21). EEC grain, sugar and olive oil prices are now well below world levels, and the export tax has been invoked by the Commission on some products. Beef prices are also now roughly equivalent to world market levels. The major residual problem is dairy products, where prices are still much higher and huge surpluses continue to grow. In the absence of effective structural reform to reduce overall output it seems that this situation will continue into the foreseeable future. However the vagaries of world markets could quickly either remove the problem entirely or, return the EEC to the position of the late 1960s with high prices and potential surpluses for a whole range of agricultural products. Such is the penalty the Community has to pay for high and stable producer prices, a reflection of the basic inflexibility of the CAP.

High prices for producers have not necessarily resulted in a satisfactory return for the farming community. Although agricultural incomes have risen since the CAP came into force, they are still generally lower than industrial incomes and show little sign of improving their relative position. The real problem is the disparity within the agricultural sector. In addition to year-by-year variations, which always affect agriculture and are part of the farmer's way of life, incomes vary, depending on where a farm is, the kind of husbandry engaged in, and the size of the unit. Farmers in parts of the Paris Basin, for instance, have incomes five times higher than those in the more remote areas of southern Italy; intensive stock farms are up to 50 per cent more efficient than general mixed farms; and units of less than 10 hectares produce a return up to three times smaller per hectare than those with more than 50 hectares.[10] In general the CAP has benefited most of those areas with large or intensive and specialized units, or a combination of the two. Northern France and the

Netherlands have been particularly favoured, but the policy is not entirely satisfactory for any single country. Regional variations have meant that certain sections of the farming community throughout the EEC believe that the CAP has unfairly discriminated against them. In Brittany market gardeners dumped their produce in piles on the road in 1972, rather than sell it at what they considered uneconomic prices, and in 1974 dairy farmers, protesting at low milk prices, drove a cow through the halls of the EEC Commission building in Brussels. There is a widespread feeling that 'the fair standard of living for the agricultural community', which was talked of in the Rome Treaty, is not yet a fact for many farmers. Unfortunately it is difficult to effect lasting improvements when net per capita value added for agriculture varies between 10 per cent and 65 per cent of that in the economy as a whole.

Another source of complaint has been the unfair distribution of the burdens and benefits within the CAP. Because of the way in which the support system operates those countries or regions that are major producers of surplus crops, that have had to be bought up by the EEC through intervention buying, have received a disproportionate share of the benefits, while the cost of the policy has been shared among all the members according to the overall size of their total agricultural industry. This has been particularly divisive, owing to the relatively small amounts spent on structural reform. West Germany for instance is not only the largest single contributor to the Agricultural Fund, it also has by far the largest domestic programme for structural reform and is forced to carry it out with minimal help from central EEC funds. In Italy, the country with the largest agricultural population, urgent reforms have remained undone, despite large contributions to the Agricultural Fund.

The discrepancies between member states where the burdens and benefits of the CAP are concerned have been further heightened by the failure of the member countries to agree fixed exchange rates for their currencies. In 1970 the devaluation of the French franc and the revaluation of the German mark seriously inhibited the free movement of agricultural products, making it much easier for the French to sell in Germany than the other way around. The unfair advantage was naturally much resented and led to the Germans threatening to impose unilateral import controls on agricultural products, thereby upsetting the whole concept of free trade. Fluctuations in exchange rates have also meant that the costs and benefits of the CAP support measures in the Community have been somewhat unpredictable. In the annual farm review prices are quoted in units of account and are often rendered totally unrealistic a year after they were agreed because of changing currency values. This problem has been particularly serious since the United Kingdom joined the Community. The £ sterling has been devalued by more than 50 per cent against the German mark since 1970 and, to a lesser extent, against all the other member currencies as well.

In addition to the internal problems within the EEC, the response given to the CAP outside the Community has been far from welcoming. Other major agricultural exporters, such as the United States, have looked somewhat askance at the unashamedly protectionist stance adopted, but have managed to contain their annoyance, because of their general approval for the EEC and its aims. For the developing countries the picture is very different. A policy of self-sufficiency in Europe has reduced non-member nations to the role of residual suppliers and, in the case of the developing countries, removed one of their major forms of export, foodstuffs. In the early years of the CAP the areas of overlap were relatively small, but since the Community was enlarged in 1972 it has been a considerable bone of contention. Two of the most difficult problems to be overcome in the United Kingdom's application to join the EEC were the need to guarantee markets for West Indian sugar and New Zealand dairy products. These were two specific issues which were openly discussed, but other developing countries without such strong political links with a member of the EEC have been less lucky and have had their trade potential severely limited by the way the CAP operates.

Rethinking the CAP

Dissatisfaction with the CAP has been widespread: consumers grumble at the high food prices, farmers complain that they still do not enjoy an adequate standard of living and politicians are unhappy that the CAP devours nearly 90 per cent of the total EEC budget. All agree that radical revision is necessary, but at the same time each group is determined to see that its own vital interests are protected. Predictably the result has been an impasse, and the history of the CAP in the 1970s has been a limping progression from one crisis to another with little or no consensus about the future role of agriculture in the Community.

The first serious attempt to revise the CAP and alter the emphasis of its policies was a series of papers submitted to the Council of Ministers in 1968, the most influential of which was the 'Memorandum on the reform of agriculture in the EEC – Agriculture in 1980'. The proposal was the work of the Commissioner for Agriculture, Sicco

Mansholt, a Dutchman, who realized that the CAP was leading to stagnation in European agriculture, rather than steady progress towards reform and modernization. The plan, universally known as the Mansholt Plan, had two basic aims: to revise the price policy so that there was a more normal relationship between the market and price trends, and to introduce radical land reform measures to bring farms up to a viable size and to enable farmers to live as comfortably as everybody else. In effect these aims were little different from those set out in the Treaty of Rome, but the new feature of the plan was the detailed proposals for the actual implementation of structural reform. Indeed the whole point of the Mansholt Plan was to ensure that the CAP in the future placed more emphasis on guidance and less on guarantees.

The Plan spelt out in considerable detail the means by which it would reform the structure of the industry. Owner occupiers prepared to give up farming were to be given grants to help with resettlement; pensions were to be introduced for all farmers over the age of fifty-five wishing to retire; agencies were to be established with the specific task of helping farmers who left the land to find alternative employment; inducements were proposed to encourage the consolidation and amalgamation of units and so reduce the number of farms; co-operative marketing schemes were to be introduced, so as to improve what in many parts of Europe was the weakest aspect of agricultural organization. Taken together the proposals were the basis for a radical restructuring of the industry, but from the very beginning circumstances conspired against their successful implementation. Although Mansholt's initiative was welcomed, the Plan itself was roundly criticized. It was argued that larger farms would only produce even bigger surpluses, that the basic ideal of the family farm would be effectively destroyed, that inordinate financial control would be invested with the EEC Commission rather than with national governments and, finally, that implementation would take so long that the proposals would have little or no effect on the short-term problems of the CAP.[11] Such far-reaching criticisms inevitably prevented the Plan from being rapidly accepted, and by the early 1970s the agricultural climate throughout the world had begun to change. World food prices started to rise sharply due to a combination of circumstances, including increased production costs and shortages caused by poor harvests in the major grain growing areas of North America and Australia. As a result EEC prices quickly became relatively less exorbitant and the cost of the CAP was significantly reduced. Expenditure on export refunds became a minor item and intervention was unnecessary for many crops, in particular wheat. The effect was to push the Mansholt Plan into the background, for despite what was said when it first appeared, the main concern in the Community was the cost of the CAP and by 1970-1 the cost of guarantees had fallen by nearly 20 per cent from the peak in 1969-70.

The whole future of the CAP was reopened after 1970 with the start of the protracted negotiations leading up to the enlarged community in 1972. The difficulties facing the United Kingdom were especially hard to overcome, since they were multi-dimensional, reflecting a combination of historical attitudes, political tradition and economic circumstance. Historically Britain had consistently refused to participate in the high food policies of most other west European countries, which had passed on the high cost of producing foodstuffs from the domestic industry direct to the consumer through retail prices. Instead it had gradually evolved a system of deficiency payments, which subsidized the producer, so that he was able to market food at prices well below the real cost. The effect of this approach on the problems of the industry had been to create a somewhat different role for agriculture in the economy as a whole. Food prices in the shops tended to be cheaper and the lower paid sections of the population were subsidized. Trade with other agricultural exporting nations had been actively encouraged in a way that would have been impossible in, for example, either France or West Germany. Finally, since the system of deficiency payments was only introduced fully in Britain just before the Second World War much greater progress had been made with restructuring the industry. The agricultural depression in the inter-war years drove many small and uneconomic farmers out of business and, to all intents and purposes, the peasant farmer, so characteristic of much of the rest of Europe, ceased to exist in Britain fifty years ago. In the late 1960s therefore, before the general increase in world food prices, it looked as though accepting the CAP would not only mean higher food prices in Britain but also the almost complete abolition of direct payments to farmers. Deficiency payments would be ruled out and because of its farm structure the British industry would not qualify for grants from the guarantee fund.

Politically there were objections to the CAP in that the British government shared the conviction of many of the existing members of the EEC that acceptance would produce a considerable transfer of power from the national government to the EEC Commission in Brussels. The British government was particularly concerned about this aspect, since it was used to exercizing a controlling interest in agriculture through the system of deficiency payments.

It was however the economic implications of the CAP which posed the severest problems for the British negotiators. As a major importer of food the United Kingdom would have to contribute very heavily to the Agricultural Fund through the import levy system, yet because of the structure of its agricultural industry it stood to gain little in repayments from the CAP. Aside from a general unwillingness to pay something for nothing, it was likely that the CAP would have a very adverse effect on the overall national balance of payments. There was much disagreement as to how great this burden would be and no way of verifying the wildly differing estimates. Basically however those in favour of joining the EEC argued that faster growth rates in the economy as a whole would more than offset the burden of agricultural payments. Those opposed to EEC membership obviously argued the reverse case. Another major economic argument was that the CAP could be nothing other than inflationary throughout Britain. Marsh, in a wide-ranging review of the likely impact of the CAP on the United Kingdom paints the following 'realistic scenario':

> First higher food prices will lead to very large wage claims on behalf of lower paid workers, to restore the purchasing power of their incomes. Second, higher paid workers will claim proportional increases in their wages in order to maintain established differentials. Third, having granted such increases in wages, manufacturers will have to raise their selling prices in order to secure a profit. Fourth in response to such higher domestic prices, imports will rise and exports will fall leading to pressures for devaluation of the pound. Should this occur the price restraining effect of imports from other members of the Community would be removed – and the cost of living tend to rise across the whole range of consumer goods.[12]

A third problem, which was common to all the EEC countries but especially acute to the United Kingdom, was the effect of the CAP on British trade with traditional foreign suppliers. Through the Commonwealth the United Kingdom had unusually extensive links with a varied and widely dispersed group of primary food producing nations and the whole complex network of relationships would be put in jeopardy by the CAP, thereby threatening the economic structure of many nations other than the United Kingdom itself. The final economic problem was the fate of certain specialized sectors of the agricultural industry in the United Kingdom such as hill farming, horticulture and intensive cereal-based livestock farming, which were traditionally heavily subsidized through deficiency payments but would have to survive on their own without special protection under the CAP.

For all these reasons the United Kingdom made much play of the fact that it would only enter the Community if the CAP was radically revised. In the event the changes were relatively minor and the fundamental mechanism of compensating farmers through high retail prices remained the same. There have been subsequent initiatives to review the whole policy, but in early 1977 firm proposals still seem some way off. As with the Mansholt Plan, the renegotiation of the CAP, which was supposedly a prerequisite for Britain's acceptance of the Treaty of Rome, has been lost in the practical difficulties of achieving agreement. Once consensus was arrived at, much of the enthusiasm for radical revision evaporated, at least as far as the Council of Ministers was concerned.

The role of the CAP in the whole structure of the EEC is somewhat ambivalent. On the one hand it represents a crowning achievement for the spirit and purpose of integration, in that national policies have actually been abandoned in favour of a single Community policy. On the other, the new policy has been extensively criticized for its high cost and lack of planning control over agriculture, making it in the eyes of many no improvement on the disparate national policies which previously operated in the individual member countries. At the level of the European Commission there is now something approaching a state of impasse: the criticisms are recognized and in many cases accepted, but there is a general reluctance to interfere too much in the only common policy that is fully operational. Not that the Commissioners and the Ministers have lacked advice on the subject. A welter of expert opinion has put forward numerous contradictory views on how best to resolve the dilemma, but the very lack of cohesion has limited the effectiveness of much of the advice.

The conflicts of interest and opinion are of course recognized by most of those indulging in criticism, and it was recognition of the need for a common view which led to a convention of agricultural experts from all over Europe being held at Wageningen in the Netherlands in 1972. The outcome was a joint memorandum which put forward five quite specific suggestions on reforming the European Community's Common Agricultural Policy.[13] First it recommended that the programme of structural change ought not to be developed in isolation but as part of a general regional policy for the whole of the Community. Secondly, it reaffirmed the intention of the Treaty of Rome that ways and means must be found to match resources to market requirements. Thirdly, it proposed that as part of the annual price review a concerted effort should be made to reduce grain prices relative to beef prices, so as to hold in check the cost of livestock production. Fourthly, it urged that agricultural products ought to be included in international negotiations, in particular the GATT talks, so that EEC prices were not kept out of line with general world levels, thereby upsetting the delicate balance of world trade. To this end it was recommended that export subsidies in the EEC should be rapidly phased out. Finally, the memorandum stressed the importance of mechanisms other than price support for managing the agricultural industry, and it specifically suggested deficiency payments and quantity controls as being two possible but neglected alternatives.

The importance of the Wageningen convention was the broad agreement it produced about the nature of the reforms needed in the CAP. The subsequent inaction by the Community itself has emphasized the essentially political nature of the EEC. Even in the realms of agriculture, policy-making is still largely determined by national rather than Community interests, and the battles which have to be won are essentially political not economic. Nothing illustrates this more clearly than the operation of the annual agricultural price review system since 1973. When currency exchange rates are relatively stable, it is reasonable to fix prices annually, but when they are as volatile as they have been in the past few years, major distortions can occur between one review and the next. In the case of the United Kingdom, prices for agricultural products have been determined in the review at the so-called 'Green Pound' rate, but at the end of both 1975 and 1976 this rate bore little relation to the actual market rate for the £ sterling. This largely defeated the objectives of the CAP, since the fixed prices were no longer directly comparable with production costs. The Community's failure to grasp this problem and to deal with it is symptomatic of its lack of political teeth and highlights a fundamental weakness in its ability to manage economic problems.

The Common Transport Policy

'A common transport policy is an aim of the Rome Treaty, but relatively little has been done to give practical effect to the principles laid down in the Treaty.'[14] This bald statement of fact in *European Community*, the EEC Commission's own journal, in January 1972, reflects an almost total failure among the six member governments to agree on how to implement a common transport policy. Whereas the early negotiations about the CAP were distinguished by a singleminded determination to reach accord, discussions about the Common Transport Policy (CTP) have been notable only for their brave words and subsequent lack of action. The contrast is all the more surprising, given the many similarities between the organization of transport and

agriculture in Europe. The recent history of both has been character-
ized by widespread government interference and management. In
continental Europe all transport, and especially the railways, has
tended to be looked upon as a public service rather than an industry
that should make a profit in its own right. The concept of even trying
to organize transport along profitable lines in the normally accepted
sense is somewhat alien. Yet transport costs form a significant component of total costs in virtually every sector of the economy, and the
problem for the EEC is that it is almost impossible to create the
conditions for equal competition in other spheres while significant
variations persist in the level and nature of transport subsidies.
Unfortunately traditional national attitudes are deeply entrenched,
and transportation itself has assumed a number of new dimensions in
the 1960s and 1970s which have challenged accepted dogma and made
compromise more difficult.

The Treaty of Rome related to a view of transport dominated by
the railways, with inland waterways an important though declining
force and road haulage an essentially local facility, with only a small
international role. Since 1958 transport has developed what Despicht
has called a 'new ecology'.[15] The pre-eminence of the railways has
been challenged by a combination of improved methods of handling
cargo in transit and the introduction of new forms of transport.
Probably the most significant of these changes is the unit load.
Traditionally transport has been multi-functional, with every carrier
being expected to be able to adapt to whatever cargo was offered to
him. It meant that not only were wagons and lorries rarely purpose
built for particular categories of freight but also that transference
from one form of transport to another was costly both in terms of
time and energy. Two innovations have radically improved this
inefficient state of affairs. The railways have introduced liner trains
with purpose-built wagons for particular goods and even particular
firms, so that they can be loaded and unloaded more quickly and
easily in the factory or at the warehouse. The second innovation is the
container, which can carry a wide range of products in what amounts
to a box with standardized external dimensions. This not only eases
the problems of loading and unloading on the railways, it also permits
quick and cheap transferability between the different modes of
transport. The same container can be hoisted by crane from a lorry,
to a train, to a boat, to a barge and back again with only minimal
delay and at low cost, thus not only speeding up overall movement but
also making the integration of the different forms of transport into a
single system much more feasible.

The impact of containers has been particularly apparent on inland waterways and road haulage. River barges are ideally suited to carrying large numbers of containers, and traffic in France, West Germany, Belgium and the Netherlands, the EEC countries with extensive inland waterways, has risen sharply since 1958. In West Germany for instance over 50,000 million tonnes/km were carried in 1974, as compared with 33,000 million tonnes/km in 1958. In the Netherlands the proportional increase is even larger, rising from under 20,000 million tonnes/km to over 30,000 million tonnes/km in the same period. In the case of road haulage the transformation has been even more dramatic: the volume of traffic in the Community as a whole more than doubled between 1958 and 1974 and now equals the railways as the most important freight carrier. Nor is it only the volume of business that has increased. Through the 1960s and 1970s road haulage has graduated from the role of local carrier to become a major force in international freight movements in Europe, with huge purpose-built container lorries carrying up to 42 tonnes. The reason for the boom is of course the flexibility of road transport. Door to door deliveries are the ideal for all forms of transportation and are easiest to achieve with lorries. Previously low carrying capacity had reduced the attractiveness of road transport, but once the so-called Eurolorries came on the market this disadvantage was much reduced.

Technological breakthroughs have not only been limited to the established carriers, and the reorientation of European freight movements owes just as much to the general introduction of new forms of transport. In the late 1950s national airlines in Europe provided prestige travel for the select few and had virtually no stake in freight handling. In the later 1970s they rank with road and rail as the main means of international passenger transport, and the volume of cargo they handle is growing every year. The change reflects a steady fall in the relative cost of air transport, due to even larger aircraft and other technological advances. In 1957 a Viscount carried 54 passengers and the single fare from London to Brussels was £8·08; in 1975 a Boeing 747 jumbo jet carried 360 passengers and the same single fare was £35.50. Similarly, pipelines carrying oil and other petroleum products, insignificant in the 1950s, had by the mid-1970s become the dominant means of transport, exerting a major influence on the locational pattern of petro-chemical industries. In West Germany, for example, heavy industry has traditionally been tied to the coalfields in the northwest; the southern states of Bavaria and Baden Württemberg have been rural and relatively backward. In the 1970s a network of pipelines links the south with ports in the Mediterranean, bringing oil direct to Munich, Ingolstadt and Stuttgart, and this has transformed the southern Länder into one of the fastest growing industrial regions in the whole of Europe.

The enlargement of the EEC in 1972 further altered the balance between the various forms of transport in the Community. There was no reference to merchant shipping in the Treaty of Rome and, since the combined fleets of the original six members only made up about 15 per cent of the world total, this was no great omission, especially since most of the ships were not involved in coastal shipping. The accession of Eire and the United Kingdom changed the situation considerably. Not only were both islands and therefore deeply dependent on local shipping, the United Kingdom in its own right controlled nearly 20 per cent of the world merchant fleet. Thus any common transport policy which ignores shipping is excluding a major element in the whole system of European transport.

For all these reasons the original conception of the CTP has never lived up to the realities of the European transport situation and, in any case, any impetus to change that conception has always been muted, because of the success of organizations other than the EEC in international transport planning. National road, rail and canal networks were mostly built during periods when competition from other European countries, not to mention the threat of invasion, posed serious threats. Once international co-ordination of economic development became a realistic goal after the Second World War, the lack of integration between the various national networks was a serious impediment to future progress and immediate steps were taken to remedy the situation.

Historically the first body set up to manage European transport at an international level was the Central Rhine Commission, established in 1815 at the Congress of Vienna to regulate shipping on the Rhine. The Commission guaranteed freedom of navigation for vessels and cargoes from any country along the length of the waterway. After the First World War, it was kept in existence under the terms of the Treaty of Versailles, but with the United Kingdom, Belgium and Switzerland as members, in addition to France, Germany and the Netherlands. In 1963 a new treaty was signed by the same nations reconstituting the Central Rhine Commission as an independent body completely separate from either the EEC or its transport policy.

The other moves towards European agreement on transport issues all date from after the end of the Second World War. In 1945, as an emergency measure, the Allies, including the Soviet Union, Czecho-slovakia, Poland and Yugoslavia, established the European Central Inland Transport Organization with an initial life of two years, to reconstruct and reorganize the transport systems in the war-torn continent. It worked very effectively, although its main successes were in returning and reallocating rolling stock which had become mis-placed through the experiences of the war. Despite its limited practical achievements and its short life-span, Despicht considers that 'it must still be regarded as the launching pad of European integration in transport'.[16]

Subsequent steps were all taken within the wider context of social and economic co-operation in western Europe. The United Nations Economic Commission for Europe set up an Inland Transport Com-mittee in 1947, with the specific task of co-ordinating transport policies among member nations. It was a clear recognition of the crucial role of communications in achieving integration and of the damaging potential of disparate and uncoordinated national policies. The record of this committee is one of solid, though often unspectacu-lar success. It planned the E-route motorway system which now links western Europe; it made provision for easier international travel, by easing restrictions on insurance cover and by introducing a voucher system for lorries carrying loads across frontiers; it also presided over a whole series of bilateral treaties which fixed quotas for road transport and enabled goods to move as freely by road in Europe as they had traditionally done by rail and inland waterway. The approach adopted was one of achieving limited objectives through painstaking negotiation; the futility of the grand gesture was always recognized and no attempt was made to undermine national transport planning.

The EEC was therefore faced with a dilemma when it came to consider its CTP, for not only was the whole field of transport in a state of flux there was already another pan-European organization successfully established, to which all the Community members were affiliated. The Commission's solution was a broad declaration of intent to dismantle existing national policies and replace them with a single new CTP. The proposal met with instant opposition and, despite agreement in principle on standard operating procedures, no real progress was made towards implementation. It was not until after the three Communities had been merged in 1967 that a concrete programme was agreed and since then limited developments have occurred. As a contribution to the broad goal of giving free access to all markets within the EEC a system of licences has been inaugurated,

giving road haulage operators unlimited rights to undertake international journeys. The system does not however allow operators to
compete in national markets and the total number of licences is still
only about 1,500, making their impact insignificant in comparison
with the progress achieved under the Inland Transport Committee's
bilateral treaties. The only other notable developments have been the
moves towards harmonizing competitive conditions. Prior to the
intervention of the EEC no member country made any attempt to
distinguish between the public service and competitive aspects of its
transport operations. This was particularly significant where the
railways were concerned and led to widely divergent and largely
unknown levels of subsidy. In such a situation true competition was
impossible, but now it is obligatory for each member country to
adopt an accounting procedure that separates out its public service
obligations. There has also been some limited success in standardizing
the basis for vehicle taxation and in creating uniform working conditions for drivers, but the sum total of these moves has had very
little impact on the structure of transport operations in Europe. The
fragments that make up the CTP at present have hardly begun to
tackle the problem: transportation remains the preserve of national
governments and private enterprise.

Regional Policy

One of the main attractions of the European Community for both the
original six members and the three that joined later in 1972 was the
promise of increased prosperity and an end to divisive regional
economic disparities. In the preamble to the Treaty of Rome it was
clearly stated that Community policies should be designed in such a
way that they would lead to a progressive ironing-out of regional
inequality. Yet, despite this commitment and the general encouragement of the individual members themselves, the Community has been
slow to develop its own regional policy.

The absence of Community initiatives is somewhat surprising in
view of the fact that all the individual members have active national
regional policies, some of which have been developed over several
decades. In the United Kingdom, for example, a regional economic
policy, in some form or other, has been part of the social and economic fabric of the country since before the Second World War. In
1973 the OECD noted that 'most, if not all member countries are at
one in agreeing that regional policies, however defined, are a necessary
element in the context of general economic policies for growth and

progress'.[17] In a later report the same organization also recognized that while there were important differences between the policies of member countries the problems they were trying to solve were essentially the same and could be summarized under three headings:

(1) The regional implications of national development policies, which affect regions differently according to their potentialities and their needs.
(2) The regional distribution of population compatible with various national objectives such as economic viability and acceptable economic, social and environmental conditions in the country as a whole.
(3) The balance of economic and social conditions requisite for equitable treatment of the populations of the diverse regions.[18]

The apparent lack of interest of the Community in these problems cannot be explained by arguing that they are essentially national as opposed to international in character. As Clout has pointed out, it is often political rather than economic considerations that have dictated how the problems are delimited spatially.[19] In many of the frontier regions in the Community a common approach to economic problems on both sides of an international frontier would be of benefit to all concerned. Burtenshaw has cited the problems created by frontier regions as a major impediment to greater unity within Europe.[20] As an example, he refers to the considerable economic discrepancies either side of the Franco–German border in the Saar–Lorraine region which have caused cross-frontier movements of labour on an undesirable scale, to the detriment of both France and West Germany.

To imply that the European Community has made no attempt to address itself to any of these regional problems would be unfair. A number of its policies have an important regional content. The guidance section of the CAP has already been discussed, as have the payments from the Social Fund of the ECSC for retraining and redeploying redundant labour from the coal and iron and steel industries. The most important contribution to regional policy in the early years of the Community was made by the European Investment Bank. Proposed in the Treaty of Rome itself, the bank was set up specifically to help finance development projects in less developed regions and other projects of mutual interest to member states which were beyond the resources of a single member government. In the event 75 per cent of the £2 billion loaned between 1958 and 1976 has been allocated to regional development schemes. Locally the European Investment Bank has made a substantial contribution to development, notably in the Mezzogiorno of southern Italy in the 1960s. However, as Holland has pointed out, it is a bank rather than a regional aid agency.[21] It is only able to offer concessionary rates of interest on loans, and there is no question of it providing investment grants or other more substantial incentives. The Commission has also proved unable to exercise much control over the choice of investment projects, or the way in which the money has been used once granted. In the Treaty of Rome it was envisaged that it would have a controlling interest, but in practice individual governments have always insisted on the right to use the money as they thought fit and, in consequence, ruled out the European Investment Bank as the basis for a Community-wide regional development agency.

The desirability of an EEC regional policy was widely recognized, as were the shortcomings of the fragmentary measures described above, but political dissension made practical progress very difficult. However, when the three original Communities were merged in 1967 the Commission set up a Directorate General to deal with the whole range of problems encompassed by a regional policy and specifically to co-ordinate the existing effort. In the event little of consequence emerged and it was not until 1971, with the negotiations to enlarge the EEC, that regional policy really became a live issue. The British in particular were determined that a regional development fund should be set up to compensate them for the costs they thought they would have to bear as a result of participation in the CAP. They succeeded, for one of the results of the Summit Conference of Heads of State, held in Paris in October 1972, was a firm commitment that such a fund would be set up within the next year.

The extent of the economic disparities within the Community are considerable and have proved difficult to remove at a national, let alone an international level. Income differences of up to 600 per cent have been recorded between the wealthiest regions of the EEC in the industrial zone around the lower Rhine, and the poor agricultural areas at the extremities of the Community, in Eire and southern Italy. In the United Kingdom, where regional policies have operated in some form or other since before the Second World War, the disparities are smaller, but have still proved relatively unyielding, despite a barrage of remedial measures. In fact the EEC, with no co-ordinated regional policy as such, has had rather more success in reducing the gap between rich and poor regions than the United Kingdom. In all six of the original member countries the differences measured in terms of income per head have been reduced, but in most cases not sufficiently to remove the regional problem. Holland and Drewer describe the situation in the following terms:

It is clear that, in general, the gap within each country has been closing, and that growth within every region has been impressive. This does not mean that the regional problem has been solved, however, as the relative differences between the main regions of the Community are still substantial. To keep things properly in perspective it should be noted that the ratio between the richest and the poorest regions of Italy is 3 to 1 and if northern Germany and Ireland are compared the gap is even larger.[22]

The Regional Development Fund was eventually announced with a great fanfare in May 1973 by George Thomson, the Commissioner responsible for regional affairs. His report proposed that 2,250 million units of account should be invested in regional projects over the next three years and precise criteria upon which selection would be based were laid down.[23] No area was eligible unless its gross domestic product was below the EEC average, or it was heavily dependent on agricultural employment or employment in a declining industry, or had a persistently high rate of unemployment, or heavy net emigration. Even then only certain types of development qualified. Projects had to be in the industrial or service sections, be aimed at creating or maintaining jobs and require more than 50,000 units of account. The Fund could only contribute 15 per cent of the total cost of industrial projects and even then the contribution was not allowed to exceed 50 per cent of the amount granted under the national regional aid programme. For investment in infrastructure, such as roads, railways, electricity supplies, sewerage and the like, the Fund could contribute up to 30 per cent of the public expenditure.

The areas eligible for these grants are extensive (Figure 22), covering all of Ireland, most of upland Britain, the western third of France, large parts of northern Germany and Denmark, all but the northern industrial zones of Italy and much of the old or industrial regions of eastern France, Belgium and western Germany. In practice the regions that qualify can be broken down into four distinct groups. First are the depressed agricultural regions, where farm structure is poor, with too many people chasing too little land, resulting in unemployment and migration. Areas such as western Eire, southern Italy, western France, Schleswig–Holstein and highland Britain clearly fall into this category. The second group are the older industrial regions which were at the spearhead of the nineteenth century industrial revolution but which have since been left behind by new technologies, less dependent on coal and domestic steel. The industrial conurbations of northern England, Wales, Nord/Pas de Calais and Lorraine in France, Wallonia in Belgium and the Ruhr in Germany are all in this category. There are then two groups of regions that are

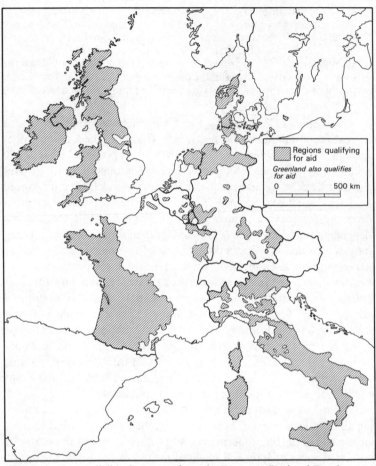

Figure 22   Areas eligible for grants from the European Regional Development
Fund since 1973

physically isolated from the main centres of economic activity, either
by geography or political chance. The extreme examples of the
geographically isolated regions are southern Italy and Eire although
other areas also suffer isolation to a greater or lesser extent. The
politically isolated regions are mainly in the eastern section of West
Germany along the border with East Germany and Czechoslovakia.
The division of Europe after 1945 cut these areas off from large
sections of their hinterland and successive German governments have
given them aid. It was clearly decided that this principle should be
continued by the Regional Development Fund.

The Regional Development Fund is not by itself a substitute for a fully blown regional policy. In many ways it is best viewed as just another weapon in the somewhat paltry armoury of regional instruments that the EEC has been building up ever since the Treaty of Rome was first signed in 1958. There has been considerable difficulty in distributing the funds allocated to it, owing to political disagreement within the Community, and its scope is very limited in comparison with the huge sums devoured each year by the CAP.

The fundamental problem is a lack of conviction. The driving force behind the Treaty of Rome was a belief that a free market with the minimum of restriction on the movement of goods and services was the most healthy foundation for economic success, as much in the regions as in the Community as a whole. In fact many economists now firmly believe that the whole policy of free movement, especially as it has influenced labour migration, has seriously exacerbated regional economic discrepancies.[24] Nevertheless, unless there is a radical change of philosophy, and unless individual member countries overcome their reluctance to see any major extension of the Commission's financial powers, a common regional policy, like the guidance section of the CAP, the Common Transport Policy, and the illfated Common Energy Policy, is unlikely to make anything more than token headway.

9

The Future of Europe

The Changing Context

The confrontation between the USA and USSR dominated Europe in the period after 1945 and made a fundamental rethinking of the continent's political infrastructure an absolute necessity. The new ideological divide ruled out many traditional alliances on the one hand and, on the other, drove countries which historically had had little in common into each others' arms. The existing national scale of decision-making was simply too circumscribed and divisive to cope with the social and economic realities with which it was faced. There was no option but to modify and replace it with a system that would allow groups of countries to speak with a single voice on major issues. All the organizations discussed in this book were set up in an attempt to create this much needed international framework. Naturally changes of such magnitude were bound to have a profound effect on patterns of geographical activity and, already, the new international and supranational bodies have transformed the spatial context within which Europe and Europeans have to operate.

The basic structure of the new order is now well-established, and the next few years are likely to be marked by consolidation rather than new major international initiatives. Nevertheless the membership of some organizations, in particular the European Community, will almost certainly be substantially enlarged, and this in itself will bring about important changes of policy and emphasis. It has already been agreed that Greece should be allowed to join, and applications are pending from both Spain and Portugal, with Turkey almost certain to follow suit. If all these countries do become members, then the European Community will become a very different kind of

178

organization. No longer will it include only the rich and powerful industrial nations of western Europe, all able – or at least supposedly able – to compete on equal terms in a free market. In many respects the economic problems of the new applicants are more akin to those of countries in the developing world, and Community policies will have to be modified accordingly. Almost inevitably a two-tier structure, based on economic performance, will emerge, and even if this is only a temporary transitional stage it will still represent a major shift from the basic philosophy behind the Treaties of Paris and Rome.

Elsewhere in Europe, the prospects for immediate change at the international level seem rather more remote. Both NATO and the Warsaw Treaty Organization are firmly entrenched as the defensive pillars of western and eastern Europe respectively. In the 1960s the continued relevance of both organizations was seriously questioned, but in the later 1970s it is generally agreed that détente must proceed from a position of strength and their future seems assured. The future of Comecon is less certain. Unlike the European Community, it has a relatively weak institutional base and almost no legislative powers, and this means that the health of the organization depends on the energy infused into it by the member governments. Bursts of activity have been followed by periods of almost total silence, but the very nature of Comecon means that it can be revived almost at will. Although currently going through a rather quiet period, Comecon may well emerge as an important force in eastern Europe in the future. EFTA too could be revived without a major legislative up-heaval, if the occasion warranted, but the presence of the European Community makes this a somewhat remote possibility.

The existence of so many European organizations does not of course automatically preclude future new initiatives, even though such developments seem unlikely in the immediate future. Among the four Scandinavian countries there have been repeated attempts to forge closer economic and political links, stretching back to the setting-up of the Nordic Council in 1952. In 1969 the governments of Denmark, Finland, Norway and Sweden all accepted a draft treaty establishing the Organization for Nordic Economic Co-operation (Nordec), which contained provision for a Nordic Customs Union, similar to the Benelux Union. So far, however, this proposal, along with many others for closer co-operation within Scandinavia, has not been implemented and Nordec as an economic entity does not yet exist.[1] Other examples are even more speculative at the present time, but it is almost certain that the potential for rearranging Europe's political mosaic is far from being exhausted.

Redistributing Political Power

The political implications of the growth of international and supranational government in Europe go far beyond simple changes in the
decision-making process at the national level. Pinder, in a survey of
future economic, social and political trends in western Europe, concluded: 'Whether . . . (one) looked at the problems of deprived groups,
or of distressed regions, or of pollution and waste, or of alienation
from work, . . . the three leading institutions of the modern economy –
the national government, the big firm and the big union – cannot
solve them without some radical changes in the distribution of
power.'[2] Even though a radical restructuring can now be seen as inevitable, it was hardly discussed and certainly not recognized publicly,
when the major new European organizations were being established.

The trends in the general redistribution are confused. In many
respects centralization has been the dominant underlying movement,
yet calls for exactly the opposite policy of greater decentralization,
have been growing in intensity and seem destined to receive increasingly serious attention from politicians of all persuasions. In the
1950s and early 1960s the balance of public opinion was heavily in
favour of centralization. The forces behind this trend have been
described with great clarity by Sharpe in a study sponsored by an
organization, Plan Europe 2000, set up to examine the likely future
of Europe.[3] He argues that the centralization of political decision-
making was encouraged by two fundamental but largely unrelated
developments in the post-war world. First of all there was the rapid
economic expansion of the two super-powers, the USA and the USSR.
Both countries enjoyed phenomenal economic and political success in
the twenty years after 1945. The government of both countries
became increasingly centralized over this period, and at the same time
they experienced unprecedented economic growth and relatively
stable societies. The inference that the one fed the other was almost
inescapable. The trend was also self-reinforcing. The enormous
economic success inevitably brought with it demands for more even
distribution of wealth and greater social and economic equality. This
stimulated growth at the centre even more, for if services such as social
services, education and medical care are to be provided equally to a
whole nation, then it requires a huge bureaucracy to administer them
and a level of finance normally beyond the scope of local resources.
The growth of this bureaucracy and the general expansion of tertiary
service industries also demanded that a growing proportion of the
population be concentrated in urban areas, leading to what Elkins has

graphically described as the urban explosion and to a state of affairs where, at a conservative estimate, 65 per cent of Europe's population live in towns and cities.[4] Centralization has also affected the primary and secondary sectors of the economy. Industry has repeatedly tried to rationalize its operations into larger units, and government has played an increasingly direct role in its operations, both as an investor through the nationalization of key sectors and as a customer for its products. Indeed the size of the public sector market and the cost of developing new products are both now so large that it is inevitable that central government, at either a national or an international level, will invariably play a key role in forward planning and management. For reasons such as these the pressures for greater centralization have been almost irresistible and seem likely to persist in the foreseeable future.

Probably just because the economic pressure to centralize is so great, the calls by the general public for a greater measure of decentralization in decision-making have rarely been louder. Individuals have come to feel increasingly alienated from the formal political process and have begun to demand a greater say in the way their affairs are determined. Almost all the countries of Europe have recently re-examined or are re-examining their local government structures, with a view to making them more efficient and responsive to local needs. The extent of the reforms and revisions in progress are well documented in the report of a conference sponsored by the International Union of Local Authorities held as long ago as April 1969.[5] The report showed that regional government, acting as a bridge between the national and local levels, would be introduced almost universally in Europe in some form in the next decade. In some countries, such as West Germany the structure is already well-established; in others, such as the United Kingdom, it is still a matter of debate as to what form it should take, though not whether it should exist.

Without doubt the demand for regional government is a direct outcome of the regional economic policies which most European governments have been compelled to pursue as part of their efforts to achieve greater social and economic equality. Increasingly the recipients in the regions have come to resent central government handouts, which have done little to alter their relative economic position. Some years ago McCrone showed that regional policies in the United Kingdom had done little to alter the fundamental distribution of wealth in the country, and the experience elsewhere has been similar.[6] There is little wonder therefore that the regions themselves have begun to demand greater autonomy in administering their own affairs. As Donnison has pointed out in a rather terse commentary on the Kilbrandon Commission's Report into the Constitution of the United Kingdom, there is little likelihood that acceding to such demands for greater regional self-determination will have much effect on the basic economic grievances which generate them, but such a prospect has done nothing to quench the demand for regional government, either in the United Kingdom or elsewhere in Europe. Lack of investment in Scottish and Welsh industry, for example, seems unlikely to be remedied by setting up regional assemblies in either country; but unquestionably their isolation from the main centres of political and economic decision-making in Europe does mitigate against them and makes the difficulties they have to face that much harder.[7]

Whatever the eventual outcome of these arguments about the redistribution of political power, it is certain that the number of levels of government in Europe will eventually have to be reduced and the whole administrative structure simplified. The establishment of supranational and international organizations has extended the chain of command at one end of the scale and the demands for regional government have introduced, or are in the process of introducing, yet another tier at the local level. In most countries the process has already begun. In Britain the whole structure of local government was reorganized during the 1960s and early 1970s, producing a very much simplified set of administrative units at the local level.[8] The process is being repeated elsewhere, but is still far from complete. The immediate future will see further considerable reorganization at all levels, and the supranational and international organizations discussed here are an important part of that process. It is fair to conclude that the establishment of bodies like the European Community started a whole sequence of administrative changes the full effects of which have yet to be worked out.

West German *Ostpolitik* and the Future of Europe

In many ways the foundations of the new Europe are still far from secure, for the whole edifice is built on the erroneous assumption that the future of central Europe in general, and Germany in particular, has been finally decided and agreed by all the parties concerned. This is not the case and, as recently as 1975, Francis Duke stated bluntly that 'the future of Germany is still Europe's central political issue'.[9] Although the Social Democratic government in West Germany, especially under the Chancellorship of Willi Brandt between 1968 and

1974, has made strenuous efforts to reach a permanent settlement with the Soviet Union and all the other countries in eastern Europe, much still remains to be done. Neither East nor West Germany yet officially recognizes the other, and the eventual reunification of the country remains officially the long-term objective of all the major West German political parties. Indeed in the 1976 federal election campaign the Social Democrat Party was forced to soft-pedal on its policies of detente with the Communist bloc and to reaffirm its belief in a united Germany.

Since the division of Germany was by far the most drastic of the political adjustments made in the wake of the Second World War, it is perhaps hardly surprising that it has been the slowest to gain general acceptance. However, the problems which it caused go deeper than a mere unwillingness to accept the demise of Germany as a single political entity. The division symbolizes the ideological split between the Soviet Union and the United States and has been largely responsible for preventing Europe from emerging as a single power bloc, capable of challenging the two super-powers on a more equal basis. As far as both East and West Germany are concerned rearmament has been strictly monitored and controlled and only allowed within the wider framework of the Warsaw Pact and NATO respectively. Technically West Germany still has no forces of its own, but rather assigns men directly to NATO. It is an anomalous situation and serves to emphasize the difference between West Germany and the other members of the Western Alliance. As time goes on, it becomes increasingly obvious, both inside and outside Germany, that one of the major barriers to a lasting European security agreement, covering both east and west, is the uncertainty still surrounding the long-term future of the two Germanies. The *Ostpolitik* and the spirit of detente, which it sought to promote, were a welcome new initiative, not only in Germany itself, but throughout Europe. They offered the prospect of the two Germanies working out a permanent role for themselves, untainted by outside interference and pressure.

The *Ostpolitik* is not a single policy, but refers to a whole series of initiatives and new policies adopted by the West German government after 1969. Most important of these was the change of attitude towards the whole of the Eastern bloc. The reunification of Germany by the simple absorption of the East Germans into a West German state was recognized as being not only unrealistic but also undesirable, as was a vision of Europe which depended on the capitulation of the Warsaw Treaty Organization. Bound in with this new approach was a more detached view of NATO. Although West Germany remained a firm

supporter of the Western Alliance, it was no longer exclusively committed to it and felt itself strong enough both politically and economically to say so. Implicit in this change of attitude was a
recognition of the impossibility of achieving reunification through the
strength of western military power. Attention turned instead to
stressing the cultural unity of Germany, and policies were designed
with a view to increasing contacts with the East German population,
rather than confrontation with their government. Another significant
facet of the *Ostpolitik* was the spirit of political realism with which it
approached its task. It acknowledged from the outset that any contacts with the states of eastern Europe could only be fruitfully
pursued with the backing of the Soviet Union, and initial efforts were
directed towards a treaty with the Soviet Union rather than the
Communist countries of eastern Europe. After the invasion of Czechoslovakia in 1968, it was clear that any other approach would have
been doomed, and this strategy had the added advantage of compell-
ing the east European states, in particular East Germany, to take the
Ostpolitik seriously, even though they had many reservations individually about the desirability of establishing closer contacts with
West Germany.

There is no doubt that the main motivation behind the *Ostpolitik*
in West Germany was political. The lack of balance between the
country's economic and political influence was becoming increasingly
irksome to both the government and the population, and with this
initiative West Germany created an opportunity to take up the
cudgels on its own behalf. The rest of western Europe also recognized
that such a development was unlikely to pose any direct strategic
threat to the Western Alliance, and it simply enabled the Germans to
enjoy some of the political benefits to which their post-war economic
success entitled them. In addition to the political arguments in favour
of the *Ostpolitik*, there were also cogent economic ones. On the one
hand, West Germany's political stance meant that the country was
effectively excluded from the markets of eastern Europe and, as
competition in the west increased, these markets were beginning to
appear increasingly attractive. West Germany's physical location in
Europe also meant that it was ideally situated to exploit both markets.
There was also the added fact that in many respects West Germany
was an economic hostage of other west European states. Always an
unwavering supporter of the European Community, the Germans
were becoming increasingly unsure whether the price they had to pay
for playing a full part in the European institutions was either just or
worthwhile. West Germany has always borne the brunt of the cost of

first the CAP and now the Regional Development Fund, and the feeling is growing that the range of economic options open to the country ought to be extended beyond the European Community.

The emergence of the *Ostpolitik* has not only been of importance for West Germany, it has also forced eastern Europe and East Germany in particular to revaluate its policy towards the west. For twenty years West Germany had pursued policies which were aimed at dissolving the East German state; the *Ostpolitik* represented a complete turnaround in the eyes of the East Germans. Not surprisingly, therefore, they were non-commital in their welcome to the new initiative. The suspicion that this was yet another attempt to undermine the long-term political future of East Germany died hard and any reaction has been extremely cautious and tentative. However, as has already been pointed out, the fact that the treaty with the Soviet Union was made the cornerstone of the whole policy meant that neither East Germany nor any of the other states in eastern Europe was in a position to reject West Germany's advances completely.

There is still a long way to go before the *Ostpolitik* will be strong enough and sufficiently widely accepted to really affect the balance of power in Europe, but the very fact that it is being discussed is an indication of the lack of certainty about the future. If it were to make dramatic progress the repercussions would be felt throughout both eastern and western Europe. The rigid division between the two blocs would be wholly or partially removed and governments, on both sides, would have to rethink the structure of their political allegiances in Europe. Defence organizations like NATO and the Warsaw Treaty Organization would lose much of their relevance, and the European Community and Comecon would be faced with a whole new range of trading options.

Such uncertainties are the very stuff of politics and they make the task of predicting social and economic trends a hazardous occupation. Nevertheless such predictions are essential, if planned development is to be meaningful. Concern about the future persuaded the European Community in 1974 to commission the Europe Plus Thirty Project. It assembled experts from a wide range of disciplines and asked them to take a look at the likely development of Europe to the end of the century.[10] Predictably they reached a wide variety of conclusions, but there was broad agreement that unless uncertainties about the future were clearly identified, planning would be largely irrelevant and the arguments for organizations like the European Community very much weaker. In other words, the future of Europe's spatial fabric is one of the keys to its geography and growth.

Notes and References

Chapter 1 *The dimensions of change*
1   A. E. Moodie, *Geography behind politics*. 2nd ed. Hutchinson 1957.
2   I. Bowman, *The new world – problems in political geography*. World Book Co. 1921.
3   R. Muir, *Modern political geography*. Macmillan 1975, p. 19.
4   H. J. Mackinder, *Democratic ideals and reality*. Pelican 1944.
5   S. B. Cohen, *Geography and politics in a divided world*. London 1964.
6   Final agreement was reached between Italy and Yugoslavia on the precise line of the border between the two countries in 1975.
7   1949, *Statute of the Council of Europe*. Cmd. 7686, Misc. 7, Article 1.

Chapter 2 *Battleground Europe and the passing of Mitteleuropa*
1   'The Allies' refers to France, the Soviet Union, the United Kingdom and the United States. Although other countries fought alongside them, they were not directly involved in the post-war political settlement in Europe.
2   R. Mayne, *The Recovery of Europe*. Weidenfeld & Nicolson 1970, p. 45.
3   E. Fischer, 'The passing of Mitteleuropa' in A. Moodie and W. G. East *The changing world*. Harrap 1956, p. 60.
4   'The Axis powers' refers primarily to Germany and Italy, although Hungary, Rumania and Finland also fought against the Allies in the European theatre of the war.
5   R. Mayne, *op. cit.* 1970, p. 47.
6   H. Morgenthau, *Germany is our problem*. Harper 1945.
7   J. M. Keynes, *The economic consequences of the peace*. Macmillan 1920.
8   M. Blacksell, 'The Effects of Bombing on the Urban Geography of the eastern Ruhr.' Unpublished D.Phil. thesis, Oxford University 1968, p. 117.
9   Lord Beveridge, 'Outlook on Germany. Part 1: The impoverishment of the British zone'. *The Times*, 29 August 1946.

Chapter 3 *The Atlantic Community and European integration*
1   R. Mayne, *The recovery of Europe*. Weidenfeld & Nicolson 1970, p. 122.

186

2   Convention for European Economic Co-operation, Article 11. *European Yearbook*, Vol. 1 (1955), p. 237. Nijhoff.
3   A. Elkin. 'The Organization for European Economic Co-operation: structure and powers'. *European Yearbook*, Vol. 4, (1958), p. 26 *et seq.*
4   See for example H. Claude, *Der Marshallplan.* Dietz VerlagG.m.b.H., Berlin 1949.
5   A. Elkin. 'The European Monetary Agreement'. *European Yearbook*, Vol. 7 (1961), p. 151.
6   J. J. Servan-Schreiver. *Le défi américan.* Editors Denoel 1967.
7   The International Monetary Fund (IMF) was created in 1945. Its aims were to promote international monetary co-operation and exchange stability among contracting countries, by setting up a fund on which they could draw, so as to cover balance of payments deficits.
8   The General Agreement on Tariffs and Trade (GATT) came into force in 1947 and consists of an integrated set of bilateral trade agreements aimed at the abolition of quantitative trade restrictions and the reduction of tariff duties among members. There are 64 members and the agreement covers 80 per cent of world trade.
9   T. Kristensen. 'OCDE – origins – buts – structure'. *European Yearbook*, Vol. 9 (1963), p. 101.
10 *NATO, facts and figures.* NATO Information Service 1970, p. 24.
11 *ibid.* p. 23.

Chapter 4   *Comecon: The Leitmotif for integration in Eastern Europe*
1   A. Milward, *The German economy at war.* The Athlone Press 1965.
2   The Cominform, founded in 1947, is the name given in the west to the information office of the Communist parties. The organization was disbanded in 1956.
3   M. Kaser and J. Zielinski, *Planning in East Europe.* Bodley Head 1970, p. 59.
4   M. Kaser, *Comecon.* 2nd ed. OUP 1967, pp. 36–7.
5   *ibid.* p. 162.
6   S. Ausch, *Theory and practice of CMEA co-operation.* Budapest 1972, p. 48.
7   M. Kaser, *op. cit.* 1967, p. 81.
8   R. E. H. Mellor, *Comecon.* Van Nostrand Reinhold 1971, pp. 111–12.
9   Anon, 'Six Nation Gas Project'. *New Times,* No. 51 (1975), p. 10.
10 R. E. H. Mellor, *Eastern Europe.* Methuen 1975, p. 94.
11 E. A. Hewett, *Foreign trade prices in the Council for Mutual Economic Assistance.* CUP 1974, p. 11.
12 *ibid.* p. 12.
13 S. Ausch, *op. cit.* 1972, p. 213.
14 M. Kaser and J. Zielinski, *op. cit.* 1970, p. 47.
15 E. A. Hewett, *op. cit.* 1974, p. 183.
16 M. Kaser, *op. cit.* 1967, p. 16.

Chapter 5   *The nature and origins of the European Community*
1   R. F. Betts, *Europe overseas: phases of imperialism.* Basic Books 1968, p. 115.
2   The Statute of the Council of Europe, Article 1. *European Yearbook*, Vol. 1, p. 275.

3   White Paper 1972. *Treaty establishing the European Economic Communities*, Article 2. Cmd. 4864, HMSO, p. 3.
4   A. H. Robertson, *European Institutions*. 3rd ed. Stevens 1973, pp. 174–5.
5   The Kennedy Round is an agreement negotiated within the framework of the General Agreement on Tariffs and Trade to promote freer trade. It was concluded in 1962 and named after the chief instigator, President Kennedy of the United States.
6   Unit of account. Common prices throughout the Community are fixed in units of account which are equivalent to the gold value of the United States dollar.
7   G. White, 'The Lomé Convention – A Lawyer's View'. *European Law Review*, Vol. 1 (1976), No. 3, pp. 197–212.
8   D. Burtenshaw, *Saar–Lorraine*. OUP 1976.
9   A. M. Rose, 'The integration of people' in R. H. Beck *et al*, *The changing structure of Europe*. University of Minnesota Press 1970, p. 192.
10 'Common Market Summit communiqué', reprinted in *The Guardian*, Monday 23 October 1972, p. 4.

Chapter 6   *EFTA: An apolitical approach to integration*

1   F. V. Meyer, *The Seven*. Pall Mall Press 1960, p. 43.
2   *ibid*. p. 50.
3   H. Rome, 'Twelve years with EFTA. 1. Austria: progress in the years of integration'. *EFTA Bulletin*, Vol. 13 (1972), No. 2, p. 7.
4   Graduate Institute of International Studies, Geneva. *The Free Trade Association and the crisis of European integration*. Michael Joseph 1968, p. 150.
5   G. Mattson, 'Eleven years with EFTA. 4. Finland – structured changes begun, but not completed'. *EFTA Bulletin*, Vol. 13 (1972), No. 4, p. 5.
6   Graduate Institute of International Studies, Geneva 1968, *op. cit*. p. 128.
7   *The trade effects of EFTA and the EEC 1959–1967*. EFTA 1972.
8   J. Walker, 'The Nordic Market'. *The Financial Times*, 2 March 1967, p. v.
9   S. Dell, *Trade blocs and common markets*. Constable 1963, p. 94.

Chapter 7   *ECSC: a pioneering attempt at supranational government*

1   R. T. Nicholls, *The European Coal and Steel Community*, prepared for the US Airforce Project Rand by the Rand Corporation (mimeographed). RM-3107-PR 1962, p. 4.
2   W. Diebold Jnr., *The Schuman Plan – A study in economic cooperation 1950–59*. Praeger 1959, p. 143.
3   Information Service of the High Authority 1956. *Towards European Integration – First results for coal and steel*. ECSC, p. 9.
4   L. Lister, *Europe's coal and steel community – an experiment in economic union*. Twentieth Century Fund (New York) 1960, p. 344.
5   *ibid*. p. 370.
6   R. T. Nicholls, *op. cit*. 1972, p. 9.
7   K. Warren, *World Steel*. David and Charles 1975, p. 154.

8   L. Lister *op. cit.* 1960, p. 13.
9   Commission des Communautes Européennes 1968. *Analyse compara-tive des structures socio-économiques des régions minières et sidérurg-iques de la communauté.* 2 vols. Luxembourg.
10 F. Vinck, 'Methods of reconversion policy in the framework of the ECSC'. *Tidjschrift voor Economische en Social Geografie*, Vol. 60 (1969), p. 5.

Chapter 8   *Common policies in the EEC*
1   J. Pinder, 'Problems of European integration' in G. R. Denton (ed.) *Economic integration in Europe.* Weidenfeld & Nicolson 1969, p. 145.
2   White Paper. *Treaty establishing the European Economic Communities.* Cmd. 4864, HMSO 1972, pp. 16–21.
3   G. Weinschenck, 'Issues of future agricultural policy in the European Common Market'. *European Review of Agricultural Economics*, Vol. 1 (i) (1973), pp. 21–46.
4   White Paper. *op. cit.* 1972, pp. 29–31.
5   H. Priebe, D. Bergmann and J. Horring, *Fields of conflict in European farm policy.* Trade Policy Research Centre 1972, p. 3.
6   A. Mayhew, 'Structural reform and the future of West German agriculture'. *Geographical Review*, Vol. 49 (1970), p. 56.
7   C. Ritson, 'The Common Agricultural Policy', *The European Economic Community.* Unit 6, Open University 1974, p. 102.
8   G. Weinschenk, *op. cit.* 1973.
9   D. Swann, *The Economics of the Common Market.* Penguin 1972.
10 Bulletin of the Commission of the European Communities 1975. *Stocktaking of the common agricultural policy.* 2/75 p. 16.
11 S. Mansholt, 'Farm reform'. *European Community*, No. 11 (1970), pp. 7–9.
12 J. S. Marsh, 'The problems facing Great Britain as a result of the common agricultural policy'. *European Review of Agricultural Econo-mics*, Vol. 1 (i) (1973), p. 49.
13 'Wageningen memorandum of the reform of the European Commun-ity's common agricultural policy'. *European Review of Agricultural Economics*, Vol. 1 (ii) (1973), pp. 151–60.
14 Anon, 'Why a common transport policy?'. *European Community*, No. 1 (1972), p. 14.
15 N. Despicht, 'Transport' in R. Mayne (ed.), *Europe Tomorrow.* Fon-tana 1972, p. 179.
16 *ibid.* p. 167.
17 A. Emanuel, *Issues of regional policies.* OECD 1973, p. 229.
18 *Re-appraisal of regional policies in OECD countries.* OECD 1974, p. 36.
19 H. Clout, *Regional development in Western Europe.* John Wiley 1975, p. 6.
20 D. Burtenshaw, 'Problems of frontier regions in the EEC' in R. Lee and P. Ogden (eds), *Economy and Society in the EEC.* Saxon House 1976, p. 217.
21 S. Holland, *The regional problem.* Macmillan 1976, p. 82.
22 S. Holland and S. Drewer, 'Regions versus Europe', *op. cit.* Unit 8, Open University 1974, p. 121.

23 European Communities 1973. *Report on the regional problems of the enlarged Community*. Commission of the European Communities.
24 S. Holland, *op. cit.* 1976.

Chapter 9 *The future of Europe*
1 R. Vaughan, *Post-War Integration in Europe*. Edward Arnold 1976, p. 95.
2 J. Pinder, 'Economic growth, social justice and political reform' in R. Mayne (ed.), *Europe tomorrow*. Fontana 1972, p. 286.
3 L. J. Sharpe, 'Centralization, decentralization, participation' in Plan Europe 2000, *Fears and hopes for European Urbanization*. Nijhoff 1972, pp. 126–33.
4 T. Elkins, *The urban explosion*. Macmillan 1973.
5 E. Kalk (ed.), *Regional planning and regional government in Europe*. International Union of Local Authorities, The Hague 1971.
6 G. McCrone, *Regional policy in Britain*. Allen and Unwin 1969.
7 D. Donnison, 'Regional policies and regional government' in M. Sant (ed.), *Regional policy and planning for Europe*. Saxon House 1974, p. 193.
8 M. Blacksell, 'A new political map for England and Wales'. *Geoforum*, Vol. 19 (1974), pp. 63–7.
9 F. Duke, 'The development of West Germany's Ostpolitik: European security and the German problem'. *Journal of International Studies*, Vol. 4 (1975/6), Pt. 3, p. 235.
10 W. Kennet, *The future of Europe*. CUP 1976.

Additional Reading

The following are a selection of books on the general theme of European integration, to which reference may usefully be made, should the reader wish to expand on the questions raised in the text. No attempt has been made to be comprehensive. So many writers from such a wide variety of disciplines have published books on various aspects of European integration that a comprehensive list would be extremely voluminous and might well lead to confusion, rather than greater clarity and a deeper understanding of the issues. I have tried to include the major works written by geographers and then concentrated on the more pertinent and accessible books by authors from other disciplines. I had hoped to confine the list to books still in print, but this eventually proved impossible. However all the books are relatively recent and should be easily obtainable through public libraries, if not in every case through bookshops.

General

R. H. Beck *et al*, *The changing structure of Europe*. University of Minnesota Press 1970.
M. Crouzet, *The European renaissance since 1945*. London 1970.
W. Laqueur, *Europe since Hitler*. Pelican 1970
R. Mayne, *The recovery of Europe*. Weidenfeld & Nicolson 1970.
A. Schonfield, *Europe: journey to an unknown destination*. Penguin 1973.
R. Vaughan, *Post-war integration in Europe*. Edward Arnold 1976.

Area studies

NATO
F. A. Beer, *Integration and disintegration in NATO*. Ohio State University Press 1969.

191

Comecon

D. Lascelles, 'Comecon to 1980'. *The Financial Times* 1977.
M. Kaser, *Integration problems of the planned economies* 2nd ed. OUP 1967.
R. E. H. Mellor, *Comecon*. Van Nostrand Reinhold 1971.
R. E. H. Mellor, *Eastern Europe*. Methuen 1975.

The European Community

J. Barber and B. Reed (eds.), *European Community: vision and reality*. Croom Helm 1973.
A. Cairncross, H. Giersch, A. Lamfallussig and P. Uri, *Economic policy for the European Community: the way forward*. Macmillan 1974.
G. R. Denton, *Economic integration in Europe*. Weidenfeld & Nicolson 1969.
I. B. Kormoss, *The European Community in maps*. Commission of the European Communities 1974.
R. Lee and P. Ogden, *Economy and society in the EEC*. Saxon House 1976.
D. Swann, *The economics of the Common Market*. 3rd ed. Penguin 1975.
L. Tindemans, *The European Union, report to the European Council*. Brussels 1976.

EFTA

H. Corbet and D. Robertson (eds), *Europe's Free Trade Area experiment. EFTA and economic integration*. OUP 1970.
F. Meyer, *The Seven*. Pall Mall Press 1960.

Population

W. A. Böhning, *The migration of workers in the United Kingdom and European Economic Community*. OUP 1972.
L. Kosinski, *The population of Europe*. Longman 1970.
A. M. Rose, *Migrants in Europe: problems of acceptance and adjustment*. University of Minnesota Press 1969.
J. Salt and H. Clout, *Migration in post-war Europe*. OUP 1976.

Agriculture

J. Marsh and C. Ritson, *Agricultural policy in the Common Market*. PEP 1971.

Transport

N. Despicht, *The transport policy of the European Communities.* PEP 1969.

Energy

R. L. Gordon, *The evolution of energy policy in Western Europe: the reluctant retreat from coal.* Praeger 1970.
W. G. Jensen, *Energy in Europe 1945–80.* Foulis 1967.

Industry

K. D. George and T. S. Ward, *The structure of industry in the EEC.* University of Cambridge, Department of Applied Economics, Occasional Paper No. 43, CUP 1975.

Monetary Union

G. Magnifico, *European monetary unification.* Macmillan 1973.
A. K. Swoboda (ed.), *Europe and the evolution of the international monetary system.* Chicago University Press 1973.

Regional development

H. D. Clout (ed.), *Regional development in Western Europe.* Wiley 1975.
H. D. Clout, *The regional problems in Western Europe.* CUP 1977.
S. Holland, *The regional problem.* Macmillan 1976.
M. Sant (ed.), *Regional policy and planning for Europe.* Saxon House 1974.

The future

W. Kennet (ed.), *The future of Europe.* CUP 1976.
R. Mayne, (ed.), *Europe tomorrow.* Fontana 1972.
Plan Europe 2000 *The future is tomorrow.* (2 vols.) Nijhoff 1972.
Plan Europe 2000 *Fears and hopes for European urbanization.* Nijhoff 1972.

Index